Brent Knoll

A notable hill in Somerset

Alan Kerr

With illustrations by Sylvia Mears

Quercus Publications

First published in the United Kingdom in 2011

Quercus Publications
8, The Barton, Bleadon, Weston-super-Mare
Somerset BS24 0AS

Copyright © Alan Kerr 2011

All rights reserved. No part may be reproduced, stored in a retrieval system, or transmitted, in any form, or by any means, electronic, mechanical, photocopying, recording or otherwise, without the prior permission of the publishers and copyright holders.

A catalogue record for this book is available from the British Library.

ISBN

978-0-9535684-8-2

Design by Noel Hetherington, Woodspring Resource Centre, Alan Kerr and Sylvia Mears

Printed in Great Britain by R Booth Ltd, The Praze
Penryn, Cornwall TR10 8AA

Preface and Acknowledgements

Like most people I have long been fascinated by Brent Knoll, particularly by the way it rises unexpectedly from the surrounding plain. A few years ago I mentioned to Sylvia that I would write an article about the hill to accompany some of her paintings. This book is that article – the subject was so absorbing I decided to write something a little longer.

I hope the book will appeal to a wide range of readers: those of you who live nearby, those of you who are visiting the area and those of you who simply enjoy the landscape and history of our country.

Researching the book has taken me on many journeys into the past and through the present and I'm pleased to share these journeys with you. But there is one journey you will need to make yourself and that, of course, is to come and visit the Knoll if you have not already done so. This is when you will really get to know a most notable hill with its magnificent views, its walks, its hillfort and its long, distinguished history.

I should like to thank the many people whose assistance with information and advice has been invaluable, among whom are the staff at the following: Somerset Record Office, Somerset Studies Library, North Somerset Studies Library, Somerset Historic Environment Record Service, North Somerset Museum, Bristol Museum, the New Room, Bristol, the STEAM Museum of the GWR, Swindon, the Peat Moors Centre, Brent Knoll Primary School and the Department of Earth Sciences, University of Bristol. I should like to thank sincerely, also, the residents of East Brent and Brent Knoll who have provided authentic local detail in my conversations with them or in my reading of their recollections.

For kindly giving permission to use material my grateful thanks go to: the Benefice of Brent Knoll, East Brent and Lympsham for photographs of the John Somerset memorial, the bench end, the Norman arch and the stained glass window; Somerset Heritage and Libraries Service for extracts from the tithe map and tithe apportionment, 1842, D\D\Rt/M/339, D\D\Rt/A/339, the extract from the East Brent British School logbook, DD\X\EBS/1 and the extract from the Enclosure Map, Q/RDE/40; the British Library for the page from John Skinner's Journal, Add. 33676, f.104, © The British Library Board;

North Somerset Museum Service for the photographs of the pottery fragments; Bristol Museums, Galleries and Archives for the photograph of the Roman coin; the New Room, Bristol, for the portrait of John Wesley; STEAM Museum for the copy of the extract from Bradshaw's Guide; Great Little Publishing for the Domesday extract, © www.Domesdayextracts.co.uk; Last Refuge Ltd for the aerial photograph of the Knoll; the proprietor of the Red Cow, Brent Knoll, for the photograph of the Red Cow; Glastonbury Abbey for the photograph of King Arthur's tomb; the National Trust for photographs of the Jubilee Stone, the slit trench and the National Trust sign.

Unfortunately I have not been able to trace the original owners of the photographs of Brent Knoll station and the ploughing scene. I am most grateful, however, to Brian Freestone and John Page for showing them to me and allowing me to use them. If the original sources can be traced I should be pleased to express my appreciation in a future edition.

A big thank you to Noel for his tremendous contribution to the layout of the whole book and to Jonathan for his meticulous scrutiny of the proof. Finally, most important of all, an enormous thank you to Sylvia for her brilliant illustrations in watercolour and pencil.

For Sylvia

Contents

1	A Notable Hill	1
2	On Top of the Knoll	9
3	The Hillfort	21
4	Invaders	32
5	The Middle Ages	44
6	Tudors to Technology	59
7	Places	72
8	A Natural Place	88
9	A Hill and its People	98

1

A NOTABLE HILL

"I have seen the Knoll"

Brent Knoll is a hill with a presence. If you have ever driven past it, and the chances are you have, you will know what I mean. In a county steeped in history, and with great natural beauty, the Knoll may not have attracted as much attention as other scenic countryside but ignored it has never been, nor ever will be. Rising unexpectedly from the flatness of the levels it has long been a focus of curiosity and a landmark for travellers.

On the M5 you can't help but notice it from either direction. Heading south it appears in front of you after passing through the Mendip Hills, and driving north it is visible directly ahead as you leave Bridgwater behind. When travelling on the A38 it towers impressively above the road.

All hills and mountains take on a different appearance depending on the angle from which they are viewed and this is particularly true of the Knoll. It assumes a variety of forms largely because of its interesting shape and the fact that it can be seen clearly from so many locations. When you drive across the levels from Mark it has a different profile to that which can be seen from Lympsham or Burnham.

A lot of people have observed the shape of this hill on their travels. I can see them now: Stone Age hunter-gatherers, Roman legionaries and marauding Vikings, followed by monks, squires, pedlars, kings' messengers and stagecoach drivers. They have all gazed at the hill as they passed by. More recently, since travelling longer distances has become commonplace, how many children, I wonder, have stared at the slopes from a railway carriage window? How many young men in their open-top sports cars have glanced at the summit whilst dashing down the A38? And how many millions of motorists and lorry drivers on the M5 have seen Brent Knoll come and go almost as quickly as a sign on the motorway? Maybe there ought to be a badge saying: "I have seen the Knoll".

It is a hill that has been duly noted by compilers of guidebooks. Describing it in the Somerset volume of his King's England series, first published in 1941, the incomparable Arthur Mee wrote that it was "a solitary hill which every motorist in Somerset knows". Writing in 1928, in his charming pocket guide to the county, S E Winbolt speaks of a truncated cone, which like Glastonbury Tor, is one of the thoroughly well-known landmarks of Somerset. The guide produced a few years later by the Great Western Railway Company refers to Burnham Level being "dominated by the lonely height of Brent Knoll, a conspicuous conical hill rising abruptly from the meadows".

Clearly for these travel writers this interesting landscape feature was worthy of mention and not to be ignored. It was something the well-to-do could look out for as they drove through the countryside in their shining new motor cars.

Living just a few miles away I see Brent Knoll regularly from my own car, as do many local commuters, but one of my favourite views of the hill, and it is one I recommend, is from Roman Road above the village of Bleadon. From here, on top of the Mendips, you can see the full extent of the Knoll with its lower plateau to the west and higher ground to the east. Resting contentedly on the flat land which has been its home for millions of years there is a calm and a strength in its presence.

An aura of mystery

I remember, once, having a very different view from Roman Road. I found myself looking at a picture you would normally find in a book of fairy tales. Below me was a sea of white cloud stretching for miles and rising from this sea was a magical island. It was the Knoll, surrounded by mist and resting beneath a clear blue sky – the perfect setting, perhaps, for a fairy story with giants in it.

And there is such a story, a legend in fact. It goes something like this. In the days when Brent Knoll was known as the Mount of Frogs three distinctly unfriendly giants lived on top of the hill. They were greatly feared by the local population and anyone travelling in the vicinity. On the other side of the Severn estuary, in his castle at Caerleon, King Arthur had just knighted a young prince called Ider. Hearing about the ogres across the water the king decided to take action and gathered together a company of fighting men, including the newly knighted prince. Over the sea they sailed, ready to do battle.

As soon as they reached this side of the estuary, and seeing the Knoll rising from the mist on the marsh, Ider decided to put his courage to the test and

View of Brent Knoll from the levels

confront the three giants on his own. He rode boldly towards the hill watched by a host of curious frogs. Mocked by his adversaries as he approached them sword in hand he fearlessly set about his task using all the skills he had learned whilst preparing for knighthood. The battle was fierce but Ider's courage carried the day. By the time King Arthur arrived with the rest of the party the ogres had been slain and their enormous bodies were sprawled across the grassy summit.

Not far away Ider's horse stood very still next to a low bank. Curled up on top of the bank, sword by his side, the brave knight lay motionless having been mortally wounded by blows from the giants' huge clubs. With great sorrow, and full of remorse for not getting to Ider in time, Arthur returned home and arranged for the body to be brought back to his castle with due solemnity. Holding himself responsible for not protecting Ider he vowed to make amends. Once again he set sail across the sea but this time made his way to Glastonbury where he established a community of monks to pray for the young man's soul. To support the monks he gave them precious gifts and also land which included the very place where Ider had fought and died so valiantly – Brent Knoll.

The story seems a fitting legend for a mysterious hill. It is a tale that can be traced back to the Middle Ages and a possible reason for its emergence in written form has been suggested by Somerset historian, Robert Dunning. During the Middle Ages a dispute arose between the Bishop of Bath and the Abbot of Glastonbury over who was the rightful owner of the manor of Brent. A copy of an early charter showed that the land had been granted to the abbey by King Ine towards the end of the seventh century but this was not apparently strong enough evidence of title. Something more was needed. And what could be stronger than the fact that the monks had been given the land even earlier by no less a person than the most noble king who had ever ruled.

According to Dr Dunning the legend of Ider and the three giants was inserted into William of Malmesbury's twelfth century history of Glastonbury by someone other than the original author. This raises the suspicion that the person concerned had adapted a similar story and added it to the official history in order to strengthen the abbey's claim on the land. In the fourteenth century a later chronicler, John of Glastonbury, retold the story changing its location to North Wales but still including Arthur's gift of land to the monks.

Once the legend had been written down the villagers who lived by the Knoll would soon have heard about it. They would have been proud of their association with King Arthur and no doubt each new generation of children listened intently to the tale as they sat around their fires at home. It is still a legend to celebrate and local people can continue to be proud of their connection with a heroic tradition that has captured the popular imagination for so long.

For many people the mention of King Arthur opens up the question of whether he really existed or not. Was there once a great leader around whom legends grew, and was this person perhaps a tribal king who organised the Britons against the Saxon invaders? In which case if he came to Brent Knoll it would have been to recruit men for his army, not to slay giants. We will return to Arthur again but for the moment we can at least acknowledge that the story of Ider adds an aura of mystery to the Knoll.

Site of King Arthur's tomb at Glastonbury Abbey

Origins of the hill

For me the biggest mystery about Brent Knoll is what it is doing here in the first place. Why is there a large hill standing completely on its own in the middle of such a flat expanse of land? The explanation for this unusual landscape can, of course, only be found by going much further back in time than King Arthur and his knights.

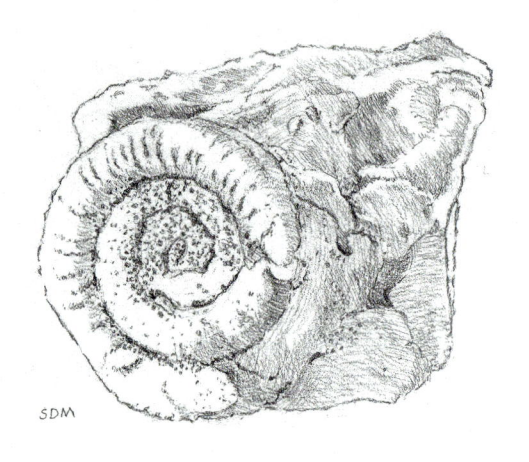

Ammonite found on the Knoll

Much easier to explain than the origin of the Knoll itself is the origin of the name Brent which probably comes from the Celtic word meaning "from a steep hill". This steep hill, like all the land we see, has been fashioned by great natural forces over timescales so vast they are impossible to comprehend. The result is a compact, isolated hill made up of a lower plateau at about 160 feet above sea level and a higher area rising steeply to 450 feet.

The underlying rock dates back to the Jurassic period which began about 200 million years ago when Britain lay further to the south than it is at present and was mostly covered by a shallow sea. Over millions of years sediment accumulated in layers at the bottom of this sea and as it was compressed it became the sedimentary rock known as Lias that forms the Knoll.

A borehole drilled on the plateau in 1971 precisely identified the strata up to this level but the composition of the higher ground has been established using surface observation. The strata can be summarised as layers of silts, clays, mudstones and shales with some thin bands of hard limestone in amongst them. At the summit is a limestone called Inferior Oolite. If a cross-section could be cut through the hill it would clearly show the different layers which would be similar to those that are so conspicuous on the cliffs at Kilve. It should be said that these cliffs are

Layers of rock at Kilve beach similar to those which form Brent Knoll

actually Lower Lias not the Middle and Upper Lias from which the Knoll is formed.

As at Kilve many fossils must be embedded in the rock but since there are no cliffs here they are not accessible. Occasionally ammonites can be discovered on the surface and they serve to remind us that the area was once submerged beneath the sea.

Knowing the rocks that make up the Knoll does not solve the mystery of why it stands alone, rising from the plain like a miniature volcano. Despite its appearance, and maybe disappointingly for some, there has been no dramatic eruption involved in its formation – just the slow accumulation of sediment. The reason why it stands in solitary splendour is not because of volcanic activity but because the surrounding rock has been eroded away by the action of glaciers.

The question that then needs to be asked is why wasn't the Knoll eroded away as well? How did it manage to defy the forces of glacial erosion when all around it the same sort of rock succumbed to the power of the ice? The most likely answer lies in the way the rock was faulted in the immediate vicinity. Where there are faults the rock is eroded more easily than where there are none and it seems that, unlike the surrounding area, the rock comprising the Knoll was not significantly faulted. So, faultless, and rock solid literally, it withstood all the forces the glaciers could bring to bear on it.

Bed of one of the streams showing the underlying rock

Today the hill rises up from the land but on a number of occasions in the past it has risen up either from the sea or from the waters of a great marsh which covered the low-lying land. The last time it was an island in the sea was only about ten thousand years ago when the melting ice sheets caused sea levels to rise. After the sea retreated the low land became marsh which eventually began to be drained and put to good use.

Over millions of years the landscape of the Knoll has been created and shaped to become the feature we now observe. From the earliest times it attracted people to live here and so begin the modern part of the hill's story – a part of the story which makes it a notable hill in more ways than one.

2

ON TOP OF THE KNOLL

Jewel in the crown

In a county full of natural and historic treasures it is easy to overlook the particular charm that the Knoll has to offer. It is an attractive and unusual piece of countryside with an absorbing history and two delightful villages nestling beneath its slopes. This is reason enough to make it a place to come and explore but there is another reason too: Brent Knoll has a treasure of its own. It is a special treasure and one that everybody who lives in Somerset, or who visits the area, should seek.

It can be found by walking to the summit of the hill. This is not a difficult walk although the final stage is more steep. The three main routes are from East Brent, Brent Knoll Church and from the top of the combe in Hill Road along the path by the farm.

As soon as you reach the summit you will find the treasure. On a clear day, all around you, stretching into the distance is a jewel – a jewel of glorious vistas that unfold in every direction across a broad swathe of land and sea. This is a place to stand and stare and this is what you will need to do in order to appreciate the full splendour of the 360 degree panorama. You will not be looking at any high mountains with snow-covered peaks, nor mighty waterfalls, nor tropical islands basking in a blue sea, but for sheer variety and interest you will have one of the finest views in the country.

Both the stones that have been erected on the south side of the hillfort make good vantage points and the viewing guide on the newer stone shows various places and how far away they are. However, to see as much as possible it is best to make a number of stops as you walk round the perimeter of the summit. Binoculars are useful but not essential.

We can start enjoying the view by looking five and a half miles to the north where Brean Down eases its way into the water like an enormous seal. At the end of the down are the remains of a nineteenth century fort where seven

Twilight view of Burnham-on-Sea, Bridgwater Bay and the Quantock Hills

powerful guns were once mounted to defend the coast in the event of an invasion. Running south from Brean as far as Burnham-on-Sea, but difficult to make out, is a long expanse of sand and sand dunes and, more obviously, a long expanse of caravan parks for the thousands of visitors who come to enjoy what local people tend to take for granted.

Close to Brean Down, Uphill Church stands on the hill where it has been since Norman times and overlooks the town of Weston-super-Mare. Weston is renowned for its piers, donkeys and mud but contains much more, especially an elegant bay and a fine architectural heritage. Both piers are visible from the Knoll. Birnbeck Pier, the older of the two, connects to an island at the end of the bay and in its heyday was the site of an amusement park that boasted a giant water chute among its diversions. The Grand Pier has been a popular attraction for over a hundred years and has recently been rebuilt with a new design after a devastating fire in July 2008. On the far side of Weston Bay is

Worlebury Hill, now covered in trees but in prehistoric times the site of a well-defended Iron Age hillfort.

Cardiff lies opposite Weston on the Welsh coast and not that long ago regular crossings to and from Wales could be made by paddle steamer. The white triangular roof supports of the Millennium Stadium can easily be identified on the city skyline. Further up the estuary is Newport, obscured by Worlebury Hill, and deep into Wales is the distinctive Sugar Loaf Mountain at Abergavenny, visible behind the Mendips above Bleadon.

The Mendip Hills extend to Wells and even further east but this lovely cathedral city is hidden away below the tall transmission mast at Pen Hill. Crook Peak rises above the motorway as it passes through the Lox Yeo valley which is overlooked by the Webbington Hotel, once owned by a member of the Tiarks family. Further along the line of the Mendips Cheddar Gorge cuts through the limestone rock of the hills not far from the reservoir which from here looks a different shape to that which it really is.

Looking south-east, thirteen miles away, is a rival Somerset landmark, Glastonbury Tor. I used to think the tor was the tower at the top – maybe I'm not the only one to have thought that – but in fact the word "tor" refers to the hill and not the tower which actually belonged to the church that was once there. Between the Tor and the Knoll is an extensive plain, mostly of pasture that until fairly recently was largely grazed by herds of dairy cattle.

To the south-west the Quantock Hills make a long, dark bank and beyond them is Dunkery Beacon the highest point on Exmoor. At North Hill near Minehead the moor meets the Bristol Channel. What appear to be two large box-shaped buildings stand in front of the Quantock Hills next to the sea. Whether they seem menacing or benign depends on your opinion of what is produced inside them as these are the nuclear power stations at Hinkley Point. The building on the right is really two buildings, the original Hinkley A power station which has now ceased production, and the building on the left is Hinkley B which is still in use. A new power station, Hinkley C, is planned for the site.

Still facing in this direction the River Parrett widens out into Bridgwater Bay, an internationally important nature reserve that attracts large numbers of wading birds and waterfowl to its mudflats and saltmarsh. At the mouth of the river is the seaside town of Burnham-on-Sea offering a choice of sand or promenade to walk along. The most prominent structure in Burnham is the lighthouse and the most energetic activity is the annual swim of one and a half miles from the beach to Stert Island and back.

Just below the Knoll spreads a patchwork of fields. They are bordered by hedges and ditches, the latter providing drainage as well as marking field boundaries. A large rhyne heads towards the north of Burnham and many other rhynes that cannot be seen flow across the surrounding levels. These are essential for the drainage of the low-lying land and, although it may not appear to be the most riveting of subjects, the way the levels and marshes have been drained over the centuries makes a fascinating story to which we will shortly return.

Gazing towards the horizon the Bristol Channel opens out to the west where it eventually becomes the Atlantic Ocean. If you flew over the sea directly west from the top of the Knoll you would reach the northern tip of Newfoundland some two and a half thousand miles away. There is much less swell in the Channel than in the Atlantic and the colour of the sea is different. It is often grey but when the sun shines it sparkles and turns to silver becoming a wonderful sight. Among the ships to be noticed on the water, sometimes moving at a surprising speed, are car transporters and container carriers heading for the docks at Portbury and Avonmouth.

Following the compass round to the north are Aberthaw Power Station and the towns of Barry and Penarth. In the distance the Brecon Beacons form the highest mountains in South Wales with the peak of Pen y Fan rising to a height of 2,900 feet. Not so distant are the islands of Steep Holm and Flat Holm, both of interest in their different ways.

Finally in the 360 degree tour we come to the railway line running ruler-straight from north to south across the levels. Stretches of it are visible as you

Train heading towards Middle Street railway bridge

look towards Burnham or Weston-super-Mare and you will not need to be a railway enthusiast to enjoy watching a sleek passenger train gliding smoothly along the track.

Whichever way you look from the top of the Knoll there is a part of the canvas that catches the eye, either close at hand or many miles away. There are hills, levels, fields, farms, villages, churches and a large river; there is a placid sea in the middle of which are mysterious islands and there is an interesting coastline. Changes of mood and subtleties of colour can be discerned and the contrast between stillness and movement makes for a pleasing effect. The stillness is in the landscape and the movement is in people going about their business mainly as they drive their vehicles on the roads below.

Much of the movement is on the motorway, one of the nation's great arterial routes. It is compelling to watch as it constantly pumps traffic through the countryside. Perhaps because I'm now used to it I don't regard it as an unwelcome intrusion. It connects us to family and friends, it brings us the goods we buy in the shops and it gives us day trips and holidays. For the most part its loud whisper speaks of the benefits it provides.

A view of the past

John Wesley, the founder of Methodism, would have made good use of the motorway. He travelled the country on horseback preaching the gospel and is estimated to have ridden 250,000 miles. On 8th September 1769, having preached at Taunton and Bridgwater, he broke from his journey to climb the Knoll and later wrote this in his journal:

> *This afternoon I went to the top of Brent-hill: I know not I ever before saw such a prospect. Westward one may see to the mouth of the Bristol Channel, and the three other ways, as far as the eye can reach. And most of the land which you see is well cultivated, well wooded, and well watered; so that the globe of earth, in its present condition, can hardly afford a more pleasing scene.*

John Wesley

John Wesley was evidently impressed with the "prospect" from the top of the Knoll. Given the extent of his travels his enthusiasm for the view confirms how special it is. The main features of what he saw were broadly similar to those of today but the detail was different: there were no modern roads to look down on, for example, and there was no railway or nuclear power station. Views change over time, rapidly when there is human intervention, more slowly when natural forces are at work.

Some very different landscapes have been observed by those who have stood at this spot during the past half million years or so. When sea levels fell during the various ice ages grassland reached over to Wales and mammoths and woolly rhinoceros roamed the plains. As the climate warmed the sea advanced and the Knoll, as we have seen, became an island on a number of occasions. It was after the last occasion this happened that much of the landscape became marsh.

It was by draining the marsh and preventing excessive flooding that the land became what it is today and looking down from the top of Brent Knoll is one of the best ways to understand how important this process was. The way the floods were tamed so that new, productive land could be created is a classic story of the struggle between humankind and nature and one that is particularly relevant to the history of this county.

Middle Street Rhyne

The most obvious examples of how the land was drained are the ditches and rhynes and since many of them were dug a long time ago they constitute a significant part of our heritage. References to draining the salt marsh and to flood prevention can be found as far back as medieval times. Sea walls in the form of embankments were erected in the area and maintaining them was given a high priority. At East Brent five tenants owed a service to look after the sea walls and a similar obligation applied to tenants in nearby Lympsham. The importance of ditches was also recognised. John Benshef of Biddisham, we are told, had to "make drains towards the sea" and do "half a day's ditching with two men".

Even with all the flood prevention measures that were taken it was not unusual for the fields and moors around the Knoll to be under water for long periods of time. In January 1607, however, a flood occurred that went far beyond anything that had ever been seen before. The sea surged over the coastal defences and reached as far as Glastonbury Tor inundating the land to a depth of twelve feet. It was a terrifying experience for those caught up in the disaster and contemporary accounts graphically describe what happened.

In one account the writer speaks of the "soden and strange cruelty" of a "terrible tempest" which struck fear in the hearts of all who witnessed the event. People were forced to climb to the tops of houses and trees, whole herds of cattle struggled for life and a wooden cradle with a baby inside was carried away on the water to be finally rescued a long way from home.

It has been argued that the disaster was caused by a tsunami but, whatever its cause, local people who were fortunate enough to see the water coming would have run to higher ground as fast as they could. Not everyone made it to safety. There are no numbers for how many lives were lost in this area as there are for Huntspill where 28 inhabitants drowned and Brean where the death toll was 26, but many people who lived on the low land around the Knoll certainly perished as they desperately tried to escape the surge.

Brent Knoll had become an island in the sea again. The view from its slopes must have been deeply troubling for the villagers who gathered in a state of shock to absorb the grim scene below. Miles and miles of brown, swirling water covered the land. Floating on the surface was a mass of vegetation together with thatched roofs, doors, fences and timber of every sort. Countless dead or dying farm animals drifted with the flow and most distressing of all were the bodies of adults and children unable to save themselves from the real-life nightmare they had suddenly been caught up in.

Contemporary woodcut of the Great Flood of 1607

The memory of that January day lasted a lifetime and the horror of it was doubtless passed on from generation to generation. But people had to live and when the water receded homes were rebuilt and farms restocked. Measures to drain the moors and marshes continued and this produced the lush, green fields that were ideal for cattle to graze on. Travelling through Somerset about a hundred years after the flood Daniel Defoe noted the "fat oxen as large and good as any in England" and commended the Cheddar cheese as being the best of its kind in the country. In the nineteenth century the county's dairy industry supplied an expanding urban population and with the coming of the railway the distribution of fresh milk to towns and cities was made possible.

Although the view from the Knoll has been one of fields and open countryside for a long time, a more industrialised landscape has never been far away. On the other side of the estuary in South Wales industrial activity has been visible for over a hundred and fifty years and on this side, too, there were signs of industrialisation. In the nineteenth and twentieth centuries the thriving brick and tile industry in Bridgwater and Highbridge was producing columns of smoke that could be seen clearly from the top of the Knoll, a sure sign that society was moving in a new direction.

Other grey and white clouds hanging low in the sky have been equally noticeable until quite recent times. These were the plumes of steam and smoke billowing from those icons of our industrial past: steam locomotives. Pulling their carriages up and down the railway line next to the Knoll they would have provided an exciting spectacle for anyone looking down from above. Not far away more steam trains could be seen on the line between Burnham and Glastonbury operated from 1862 by the Somerset and Dorset Joint Railway Company.

Developments in transport by road and by sea would also have been noticed by those who watched from the summit. For hundreds of years packhorses, carts and stagecoaches made their way purposefully along the thoroughfare below which later became the turnpike and ultimately the A38. As a major road this has been used by cars, lorries and coaches of every shape and size. Out at sea a variety of maritime traffic has passed by including Viking longships, cargo vessels, oil tankers and the infamous ships that engaged in Bristol's slave trade.

The view from the top of the Knoll is, and always has been, something quite special. It is a scene with a diverse and attractive landscape and an abundance of history. Whether you simply take in the view, or whether you reflect on all that has gone before, the likelihood is you will feel better just for being here.

Beacons and bonfires

Jubilee Stone

The Knoll is an ideal location for a beacon since it can be seen from so far away. Fires have been lit on the summit as warnings or celebrations for at least two and a half thousand years. In a sense, therefore, the commemorative stone erected to mark the bonfire for Queen Victoria's Golden Jubilee can be regarded as a monument to all the beacons that have ever been lit there.

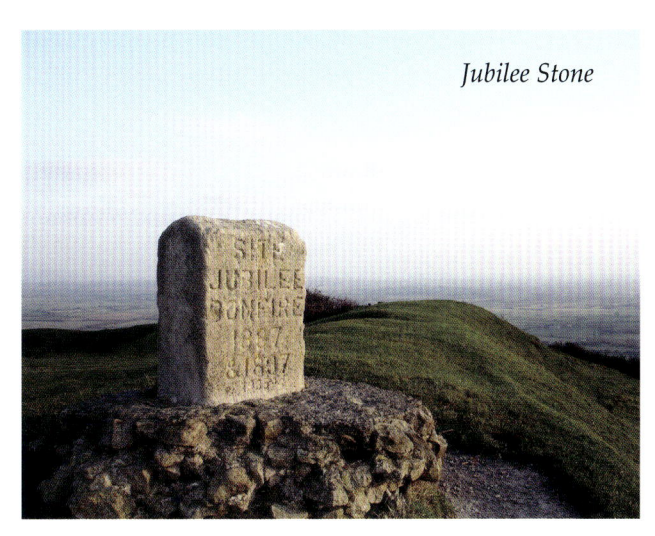

During the Iron Age especially, beacons would have been used to send signals to nearby hillforts and settlements. Smoke or fire could easily be seen by the occupants of the hillfort on Worlebury and in the opposite direction a beacon would have been visible on the Poldens thus allowing signals to be relayed onwards into South Somerset. Bearing in mind that this was a period when tribal hostilities could suddenly erupt it is likely that who sent messages to whom using the beacon network varied considerably according to the friendship patterns at any given moment.

In Saxon times local beacons may have been used again to warn of imminent Viking raids and in the late Middle Ages they became part of a wider coastal defence system. During the reign of Queen Elizabeth 1, when there was a serious threat of a Spanish invasion, a national network of beacons was prepared for use.

Although there is no documentary evidence of a beacon on Brent Knoll at the time of the Spanish Armada we can be almost certain there was one. Well before July 1588, the date when the Armada entered the English Channel, the arrangements for the beacon would have been put in place. These included ensuring a supply of combustible fuel and organising the watchmen – paid villagers who were regularly checked to see they were at their post.

In addition to setting up the country-wide system of beacons, preparations had also been made nationally to assemble, equip and train a large militia capable of resisting an invading army. In Somerset every district was required to provide armed men ready to march at a moment's notice. Those who were selected were trained in the use of weapons and no doubt some of the local training took place on the Knoll which would have been ideal for the purpose. Musters were held frequently and the militia inspected by an official known as the Muster Master. In March 1588, obviously pleased with the quality of the Somerset recruits, he reported finding them "brave and very well furnished".

Brazier beacon

At the height of the crisis we know that two large forces of the Somerset militia were ordered to Dorset and London while the Armada was still a threat. What we do not know is whether the beacon on the Knoll was ever lit during the emergency. There is evidence that some beacons were fired, initially in Cornwall and later in Hampshire, but it seems the network as a whole was never put to the test. From the time the Armada began sailing up the English Channel Elizabeth's fleet had the situation under control and within a short space of time the threat of an invasion had passed. There was no need, in the event, to fire the great chain of beacons that had been so carefully prepared.

It was not until four hundred years later in 1988 that the full effect of the beacon chain could finally be seen. To mark the anniversary of the Armada, bonfires were lit at numerous sites all over the country – although I've been unable to confirm there was one on the Knoll.

That doesn't matter as plenty of other bonfires and beacons have blazed on the summit in the recent past. One that must have drawn a large crowd was lit on VE Day towards the end of the Second World War and another was lit for the Millennium. Earlier bonfires are recorded on the commemorative stone for 1887, Queen Victoria's Golden Jubilee, and for 1897, her Diamond Jubilee. The coronation bonfires for Edward VII and George V are also commemorated on the stone as is the bonfire for Queen Elizabeth II's Silver Jubilee.

Newspaper report of 1887 Jubilee Bonfire

> The beacon fire lighted on Brent Knoll on Tuesday evening was a grand sight. The expense was defrayed by subscription, amounting to nearly £20. Mr. W. S. Holt also gave four wagon loads of wood; Archdeacon Denison, one ton of coal and three loads of wood; Mr. J. T. Nicholetts, one load of wood; and Mr. Cuthbert Ritson, 300 gallons of creosote and 200 gallons of petroleum; making altogether a total of between 70 and 80 tons of material, which was conveyed to the top of the Knoll by Messrs. J. Isgar, T. Huett, H. Body, and W. Comer, half-a-dozen horses being required for each load. During the evening there was a capital display of fireworks, the committee setting £10 apart for that object.

All these fires would have been seen for miles around and some of them must have been truly spectacular. According to the Bridgwater Mercury the jubilee bonfire of 1887 was gigantic. It was made with 70 to 80 tons of material consisting of coal, wood, 300 gallons of creosote and 200 gallons of petroleum. As the report in the newspaper says it would have been "a grand sight".

On all these celebratory occasions the bonfire on the Knoll would have rounded off a memorable day of festivities when people from all walks of life came together with a strong sense of national pride. And if having a bonfire on top of a hill brings people together that is surely a good enough reason in itself to have one.

3

THE HILLFORT

A place to settle

For thousands of years people have stood at the top of the Knoll and quietly absorbed the views. But there is something else to absorb as well as the view. As you stand on the ramparts of what was once an Iron Age hillfort you can sense the great antiquity of the place and with a little imagination take yourself a long way back in time.

Built in about the sixth century BC, and probably modified at later dates, it is unlikely that the hillfort was the first settlement on the Knoll. From archaeological evidence found at other sites in Somerset it seems reasonable to suppose that people lived here as long ago as the Old Stone Age. I like to

Herds of deer roamed the grassland which stretched across to Wales

imagine who might have been the first person to climb to the top of the Knoll and look out across the levels. It must have been someone and the person I see is a hunter from the early part of the Old Stone Age. He doesn't belong to our own species, *Homo sapiens*, but we won't hold that against him.

As he looked around he saw the hills of Somerset as they are today but on the levels, instead of green fields and tall trees, a grassy tundra stretched into the distance. Dry land extended across to Wales as sea levels had dropped and there was no Bristol Channel.

My hunter-gatherer was not there to admire the view. He and his hunting companions, all carrying wooden spears, had a more pressing reason to survey the countryside. At their temporary camp the supply of meat was running low and they needed to find more food. From the top of the Knoll they could see if there was a herd of deer nearby which would easily solve their problem. Such a band of men, accompanied by their women and children, would surely have been the first of other similar groups to set up camps and use them as a base for hunting expeditions.

Moving rapidly through time, a few hundred thousand years in fact, we come to the Middle Stone Age, or the Mesolithic, as it is known. The climate was warmer, sea levels had risen and forests, not grass, covered vast areas of land. Living in these forests were deer, wild cattle and boar which for the most part stayed in the same locality providing a constant source of food for human beings who were there too. It was therefore no longer necessary for hunter-gatherers, now fully human, to be continually on the move and as a consequence they gradually adopted a more settled way of life.

A settled way of life led to the development of farming in the New Stone Age, or Neolithic, and it was this momentous innovation that changed the course of human history. The first farmers not only ensured that every succeeding generation would be able to provide food for their families, they began the process which led to the creation of society as we have come to know it. Brent Knoll, I'm sure, played its part in the process. Although there is no tangible evidence that the Knoll began to be farmed at this time, from about 4,000 BC onwards, there is every possibility that this is when the first small farms appeared.

Surrounded by marsh, as it now was, this piece of land may not have appeared to be the most inviting environment in which to make one's home. But put yourself in the position of a family looking for somewhere to live and its attractions were obvious. Fresh water flowed down the hill in a number of streams and plenty of food could be found in the woods which covered the

Knoll and in the wetlands close-by. On the lower slopes there was potential for land to be cleared so that animals could be kept and crops grown, and there was no shortage of suitable material to build a home. To an enterprising Neolithic family this isolated hill must have looked a promising location to take up the challenge of self-sufficiency.

I'm attracted to the idea that Brent Knoll was settled well before the Iron Age partly because of what was happening less than ten miles away. Across the marshes were thriving communities who lived at the foot of the Poldens and on raised islands in the Somerset levels. These were the people who constructed the famous wooden trackways over the marsh, sections of which have been discovered in the peat. If there were communities not far away on the levels, and also on the Mendips, there is no reason why the Knoll should not have been settled at this time.

The early settlers worked with tools made of flint. Their skill with these implements enabled them to do just about anything including felling trees and splitting their trunks, and on a smaller scale making bows and arrows. A remarkable find from the levels was one half of a longbow made of yew, dating from 3500 BC, which was no doubt used effectively when hunting.

It is probably safe to say there has been human habitation on and around the Knoll from the New Stone Age onwards even if it has not always been continuous. It is during the Neolithic that the human story of the Knoll really begins, the story of all the people who down the ages lived, worked and raised families here.

After the Neolithic came the Bronze Age when the local inhabitants eagerly began to use the amazing new product of metal. Tools, weapons and jewellery made of bronze gradually became familiar items in every household and replaced those that were made of stone.

Finally, on our rapid journey through prehistoric times we reach the Iron Age and the hillfort, and here we will pause to explore the scene in greater detail.

A hillfort to defend

Countless visitors have made it to the top of the Knoll and admired the view. One visitor, however, was more interested in what he could see beneath his feet than anything he could see in the surrounding landscape. His name was John Skinner, the Reverend John Skinner, rector of Camerton from 1800 to

1839 and previously, for a brief period, curate at South Brent – the former name of the village of Brent Knoll.

No discussion of archaeology in Somerset would be complete without mention of this scholarly and energetic clergyman who literally made his mark on Brent Knoll as he did at many other sites. His forthright opinions and overbearing personality did not endear him to his parishioners and his personal life was scarred by the death of his wife and three of his children. In later years his uneasy relationship with his grown-up sons and daughter caused him great anxiety and his deteriorating mental health tragically led him to take his own life.

The Reverend Skinner found relief from his professional and personal troubles by pursuing his passion for archaeology and it was this that drew him back to the hillfort he would have known from his time as a curate. Despite lacking the rigour of modern archaeological practice his excavations on the summit of the Knoll, and his recording of them, have provided important evidence about the distant past. Although he called the hillfort a "Belgic and Roman Encampment", which places it at the end of the Iron Age,

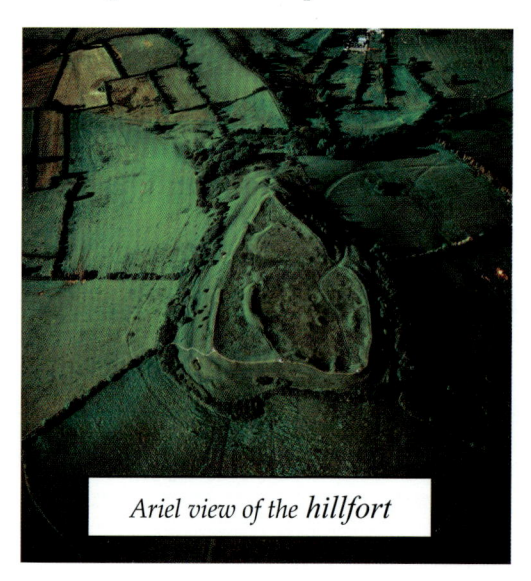

Ariel view of the **hillfort**

his discovery of a flint arrowhead persuaded him that it was settled earlier. One arrowhead does not prove human habitation but, as it happens, Skinner was right. The hillfort was indeed built and occupied well before the Romans came and, as has just been said, people had probably been living on other parts of the Knoll since the Stone Age.

Skinner unearthed a lot more than one flint arrowhead and we will look at his discoveries in the next chapter, but the most exciting archaeological evidence at the hillfort is not to be found buried beneath the soil, it is completely visible above the ground. In fact, as you reach the top of the Knoll, you are standing on it. You are actually standing on the ramparts that were built to defend the hillfort in the Iron Age and if you exercise your imagination as you walk around them you will be taken back in time just as surely as if you were visiting a medieval castle.

Covering an area of four acres the hillfort at Brent Knoll is comparatively small. The interior of the site has been affected by surface quarrying but most of the original defences have remained intact. Surrounding the whole enclosure is a low bank on top of which people now walk and this was built either with stones, or with earth and stones. Without serious investigation we cannot be sure exactly how it was initially constructed or how it may have been modified in subsequent periods.

Below the bank on the outside is a narrow terrace and dropping down from this is a steep slope of between forty and fifty feet. At the bottom of the slope is a wide, flat terrace that may have been deliberately made this way or perhaps dug as a ditch that has filled with soil over time. In order to create this terrace or ditch it would have been necessary to cut into the hillside and to excavate the slope above. This was a huge task requiring countless hours of manual labour but the end result was a highly effective defensive feature.

The main entrance is on the east side and is reached by walking from the Jubilee Stone in the direction of the Mendip Hills until you come to a gap in the ramparts. Like all hillfort entrances this would have been well-fortified and designed in such a way as to give the maximum advantage to the defenders.

The hillfort is one of many similar structures in Britain which puts Brent Knoll into the mainstream of British history where building these massive defences was common practice. In the immediate locality Dolebury and Worlebury are fine examples of hillforts and not far away South Cadbury and Maiden Castle look as formidable now as they did two and a half thousand years ago. At Danebury in Hampshire the site was excavated for almost twenty years and what was discovered has added enormously to our knowledge of hillforts and the people who occupied them. An excellent museum at Andover recreates Iron Age life at Danebury and is well worth a visit.

We have already seen why the Knoll was a good place to live, with fresh water and food readily available, but why did it become necessary to defend it with a hillfort? For obvious reasons I imagine. Society had become more settled, more territorial and more tribal. It was natural that communities felt that the land they farmed, as well as its produce, belonged to them and if necessary had to be defended. At Brent Knoll and elsewhere people built hillforts to defend their territory and protect their possessions. We cannot be certain whether the hillfort on the Knoll served only the people who lived in the vicinity or whether, later on, it also became part of a wider defensive network, but for both purposes it was a perfect site to fortify. Climbing the steep slopes would have put any attackers at a disadvantage, slowing them down and making them prime targets for picking off with sling stones and spears. Moreover, the view in every direction would have made an enemy visible at a distance thus giving the occupants of the hillfort ample time to prepare themselves.

The fact that so many hillforts were built suggests more than a passing interest in how to defend oneself against hostile neighbours in the event

Iron Age warrior with sling and pouch

of an attack. Most of the time people led a peaceful existence which centred around the daily routines of domestic life, farming and making the things they needed. On occasions, however, when trouble arose, they had no hesitation in putting their fortifications to good use. At Danebury 11,000 sling stones were retrieved from a single pit which indicates that defending one's territory was taken very seriously. It is more than likely therefore that here on the slopes and ramparts of Brent Knoll there were times when fierce fighting took place and that people died as a result.

Given the absence of a thorough excavation of the site, together with the extensive quarrying that has taken place, we can only speculate about what was inside the hillfort. With the ramparts providing some protection from the wind there may have been four or five roundhouses, one slightly bigger belonging to the local leader and the others for members of his extended family. More homes would probably have been built on the plateau below the hillfort or at the base of the hill but when the community was threatened everyone would have sought refuge at the summit. At a time when feuding and conflict were never far from the surface, having the protection, and deterrent value, of a hillfort was crucially important.

The hillfort served other purposes too. Living in an impressive-looking fort on top of a hill would have been a clear symbol of status and authority for a local chieftain and, although not in the same league as Maiden Castle, the stronghold would have been large enough to confer considerable respect on its occupants.

In addition to being a secure and prestigious location in which to live a hillfort was a place where people could meet and talk. Topics of conversation were not very different from our own. Families, homes and the weather must have featured regularly, plus what was happening in the wider world – which normally was not very wide but was nevertheless of great interest especially in times of tribal feuding. Success and failure with the crops would have been another subject for discussion as would the condition of the livestock.

People also gathered at hillforts to exchange things. They were ideal sites to use for this essential activity. Those who lived on or around the Knoll would have wanted to exchange animals, grain or homemade products amongst themselves and in addition would have traded goods with visitors from other local communities. It is possible that items from Europe occasionally appeared at the hillfort and in the late Iron Age these may even have included wine from Italy. Brent Knoll was not so isolated as we might think.

Just as people from nearby settlements travelled to the Knoll, so the inhabitants of the Knoll did their own travelling to seek out products they were not making themselves. Visits to Worlebury were probably quite common as were those to what are now known as the lake villages of Meare and Glastonbury. Here they may have acquired attractively decorated pots, and jewellery made from beads of amber, glass or shale. They would certainly have been interested in any iron implements they saw on their travels even though they were able to smelt iron ore themselves. This would have been one of the many craft skills that were important for the Iron Age community that by now had become established on the hill.

Life in the Iron Age

We don't know whether the hillfort itself was definitely inhabited but for the moment let us assume that it was. If we travel back to the past we can see what may have been happening there one day in late summer in about 250 BC. Inside the enclosure are five roundhouses spaced evenly over the southern half of the site, the one nearest the embankment being a little larger than the others. All are built in the same way with a low wall, a conical thatched roof and a doorway. One of the roundhouses is under construction

Iron Age roundhouse

and two girls are daubing a mixture of clay, dung and straw over wattles that have been woven together to form the circular wall.

Each house is comfortable, spacious and sturdy. The whole family lives and sleeps in an open space containing everything that is needed without being cluttered. For sleeping there are two beds made of reeds covered in hides and woollen blankets. One is for the parents and one for the children. There are also benches, stools and an assortment of implements including wooden rakes and pitchforks. A fire smoulders in the middle of the open space and instead of the smoke rising through a hole in the roof it seeps through the thatch gradually to prevent an updraft that could be dangerous. The interior is completely dry despite recent heavy rain which has formed pools of water around the encampment.

Outside, people are going about their daily business. An older-looking man is carrying out a repair to a plough and a muscular younger man is energetically wielding an axe to cleave a tree trunk. Close-by an attractive, smartly dressed woman stands in front of an upright loom and weaves a length of patterned woollen fabric. Her appearance is obviously important to her as she is wearing a necklace made of glass beads.

Another woman unloads fresh produce from her wicker basket. She has not been shopping but has returned from a well-cultivated plot of land on the lower plateau. A few minutes later she sits outside her house cutting up pieces of meat and putting them into a blackened pot of simmering water. Next to her a girl is engaged on the laborious task of using a stone rotary quern to grind corn into flour.

Below the hillfort and clearly visible on the lower slopes to the south are flocks of sheep and cattle. On the plateau fields of stubble can be seen where the wheat has recently been harvested but in one field a crop of Celtic beans is still growing.

To take ourselves back to a typical day in the life of the hillfort is to enter a world full of ordinary people each with a story to tell. Their stories are part of our story and that is why we are curious about them. On the whole their lives were comfortable enough even if they lacked the sophistication of

Rotary quern

other contemporary societies like those of Ancient Greece. They had good houses and a plentiful supply of food, and for the most part they led a peaceful existence attached to the land and regulated by the seasons.

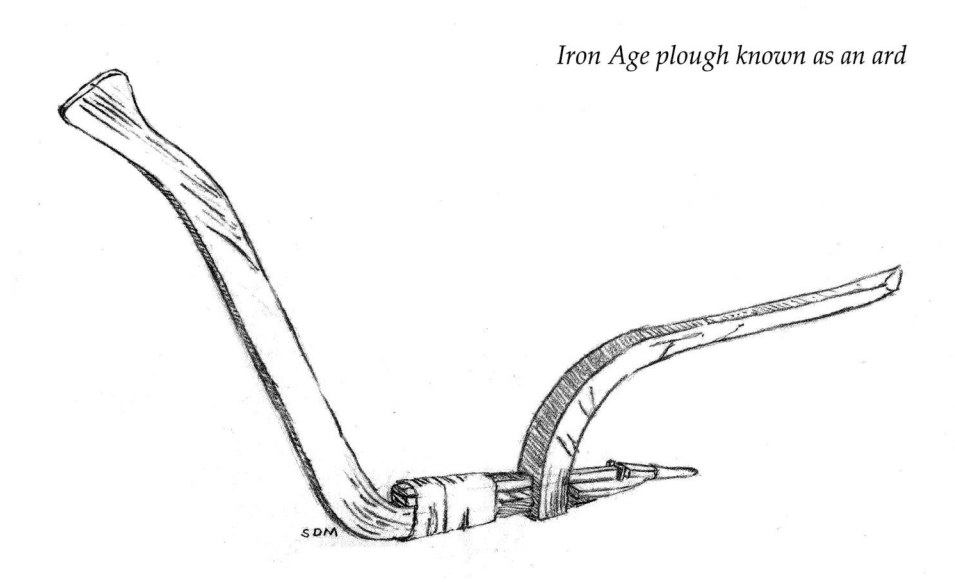

Iron Age plough known as an ard

Before we leave the hillfort we need to look along its ramparts, the defining evidence of a community that lived here over two thousand years ago. The embankment is grassed over as it is today and a wooden palisade extends all the way round except at the main entrance. Here a large wooden gate has been left open to allow people to come and go.

On this late summer's day two men patrol on top of the embankment. Both have moustaches and quite long hair. Beneath their tunics they wear brightly coloured, woollen trousers woven in a tartan effect and on their feet are leather shoes.

If their conversation could be overheard it would reveal the dramatic events of the preceding week when a rival tribe who lived on the Mendip Hills had attacked the hillfort. Shortly before the attack the young men of this tribe had carried out a cattle raid on the Knoll during which the son of the tribe's chief had been killed. On hearing the news he had demanded that the person responsible for his son's death should be handed over or he would come and seize him.

Ignoring his demand the inhabitants of the hillfort and the other dwellings on the Knoll had prepared for battle. The men had stripped to the waist, painted blue patterns on their bodies and armed themselves with swords, spears and slings. They had faced an assault from over fifty well-armed warriors and had used their slings to great effect. Unfortunately, while they had been concentrating on defending the gate, the ramparts on the south side had been overrun resulting in fierce hand-to-hand fighting. In the end the instinct to survive, as well as superior skill, had finally given the defenders victory at the cost of two men killed and a number injured.

It was at the close of the Iron Age, in AD 43 and immediately afterwards, that patrols on the ramparts and daily observations of the countryside would have been renewed. The men who were now patrolling were not looking out for the hostile forces of a neighbouring tribe but for a much more formidable adversary. The Romans had invaded and the 2nd Legion had begun its conquest of the south and west.

4

INVADERS

The Romans arrive

We can imagine how the modern media would have covered the three occasions when the Roman Empire's awesome military machine set about invading Britain. Breaking news from embedded reporters would have filled our screens and every aspect of the unfolding drama would have been picked over in minute detail. But with no camera crews to record the action, and no screens inside the roundhouses, news of the invasions would have reached the families on the Knoll some time after the events occurred. With a mix of curiosity and awe they would have listened to second and third-hand accounts of thousands of soldiers in helmets and armour stepping ashore from their ships and taking on the Britons with javelins, swords and daggers.

It was invasion number three that proved to be decisive and resulted in the occupation of Britain until the early fifth century. In AD 43 the Emperor Claudius, in search of personal prestige, embarked on a full-scale conquest. Despite serious resistance the might of the Roman army prevailed and Claudius himself joined the final stages of the campaign. However, it was a future emperor, Vespasian, who had the most influence on the immediate prospects for the Knoll as it was under his command that the 2nd Legion was dispatched to deal with the south and west. According to the Roman historian, Suetonius, Vespasian conquered the Isle of Wight, subjugated two warlike tribes, captured more than twenty settlements and fought thirty battles.

Unfortunately there is no record of the location of the battles nor of their intensity. We do not know how many hillforts were involved but these would have been obvious locations for native Britons to make a stand. It is an intriguing possibility, therefore, that Vespasian himself, or one of his tribunes, came to the Knoll to ensure that it would not become a centre of resistance.

Roman legionary of the 2nd Legion commanded by Vespasian

We will never know whether the hillfort was the site of a heroic stand against the Romans as Maiden Castle appears to have been. It may have been a site of armed resistance or it may not. My own feeling is that seeing a large force of heavily armed Roman legionaries making their way across the marsh would have persuaded local leaders to take the sensible decision not to engage in battle. Instead they may have arranged a meeting with senior officers of the

Roman army at which, one assumes, there would not have been a great deal of negotiation. The Roman delegation would have made it quite clear that from now on they were in charge and they made the rules. To reinforce the point they would have left small contingents of legionaries at each of the hillforts in the area, which for Brent Knoll and the other settlements marked the beginning of almost four centuries of occupation.

Part of the Empire

For good reason this period in our country's history continues to capture our imagination. It is endlessly fascinating to look back at the impressive achievements of the Romans and to visit places where we can see and feel their presence. There were not many true Roman settlers living around the Knoll but there is plenty of evidence of the overall effect of the occupation. This evidence is more substantial than is generally realised and includes coins, pottery from different sites, the remains of what was a temple, and a villa.

The Reverend Skinner, whom we met in the previous chapter, carried out excavations inside the hillfort on at least three occasions and discovered fragments of Romano-British pottery and a number of fibulae dating from the same period – a fibula being a brooch used for fastening. Significantly, he also unearthed roof tiles of pennant sandstone, painted plaster and foundation stones from which we can deduce that a permanent building was here, probably a temple.

No coins were found by Skinner and his diggers although they were aware of coins that had previously been discovered. One notable find before his own excavations was an urn containing coins of the Roman Emperors Trajan and Severus but these have long since disappeared. Disappointingly the only Roman coin found on the Knoll which can presently be seen is an

Coin found on the Knoll (left) and how it would have looked

antoninianus, probably of the Emperor Victorinus who ruled from 269 to 271. It was acquired by Bristol Museum in 1967 and makes an interesting addition to the body of evidence about the period.

Local people did not suddenly start speaking Latin or wearing togas when the Romans arrived. A toga would not have been a sensible garment for a day's ploughing which remained a regular seasonal task. Nor did the local inhabitants abandon their roundhouses and take up residence in heated villas

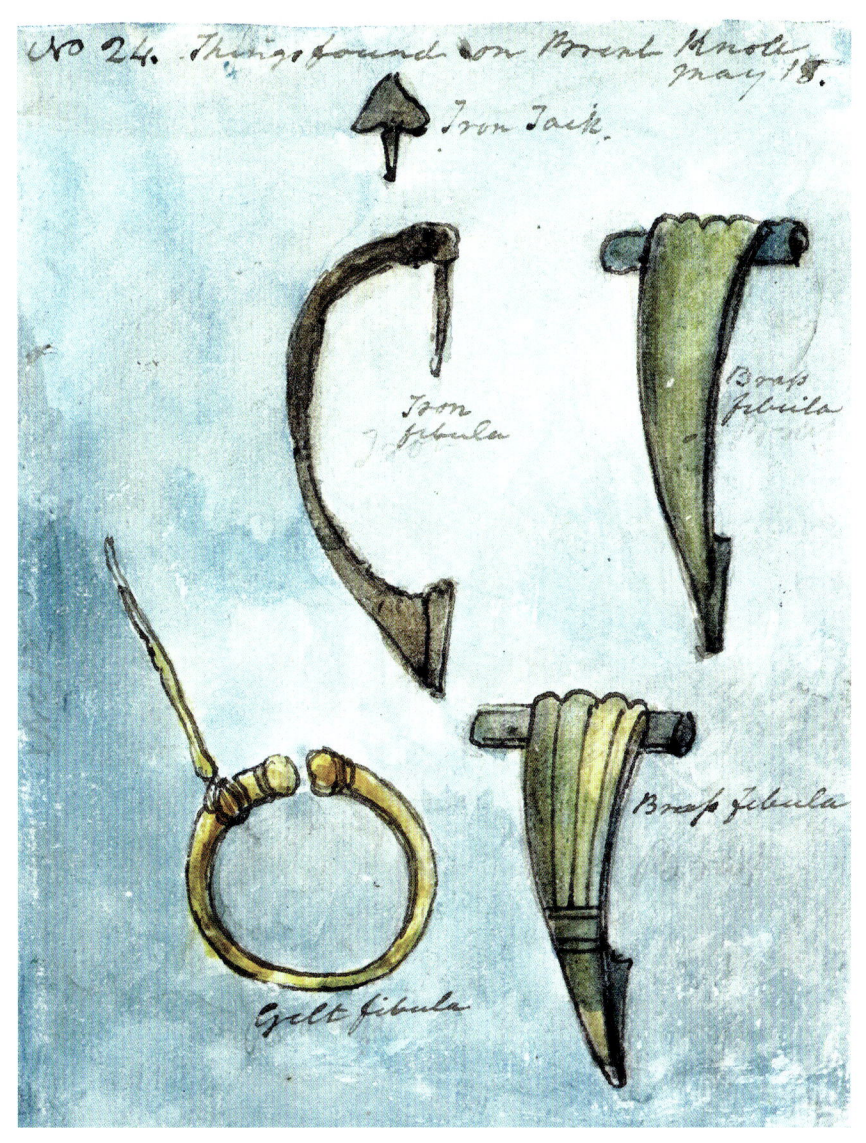

Paintings by Reverend John Skinner of some of his discoveries at the hillfort. Taken from his journal held at the British Library.

with beautiful mosaic floors. They continued to live in traditionally built homes, round or possibly rectangular, which were situated on the plateau or lower slopes but not now within the hillfort. The daily routines of life were largely unchanged. Farming and managing the land carried on in much the same way as before, as did all the other essential activities such as grinding flour, weaving clothes and mending tools.

Perhaps the most obvious difference in people's everyday lives lay in the range of produce that could be grown and added to their diet. The Romans introduced many new vegetables including onions, leeks and cabbages and a wide variety of fruit was brought into cultivation. Somewhere on the slopes of the Knoll the first apple trees could have been planted at this time.

The small farmers in the area may not have moved into a villa when the Romans came but one person did. And it was this person who brought something radically different to the familiar rural scene and made the triumphs of Roman civilisation visible to those who lived nearby. In 1970 while the M5 was under construction the remains of a Roman villa were discovered. These included dressed stone blocks and slabs, painted wall plaster, window glass, roofing tiles and other sorts of tiles that were used in the building of hypocausts. Apart from demonstrating a whole new way to build a house, the villa was also a reflection of the opulent lifestyle that some people were able to have. This was luxury that no one could have imagined before the Romans arrived. And it was right here, just below the Knoll, where everyone could see it.

The villa would have made a noticeable contribution to the local economy. The marsh adjacent to it would have been drained and the reclaimed land used for crops and grazing. Although slaves would have been employed in the running of the villa estate there were no doubt employment opportunities for the villagers either by working on the land or helping with other jobs that needed to be done.

Who did this splendid home belong to? A wealthy or powerful native Briton, a high ranking official, a retired centurion maybe, or even someone living in Rome. It is interesting to speculate. I wonder, too, what life was like for the families who lived there over the years. It was definitely less demanding than that of their neighbours with the men opting out of hard manual labour and the women leaving the housework to the servants.

For the residents of the Knoll the daily round at home and at work was much the same as it had always been but some effects of the occupation were impossible to ignore. For example, traditional forms of tribal justice were replaced by the long arm of the Roman law even if in practice some laws were observed more than others. Another effect was having to pay taxes in order to support the great empire of which this small community was a part. It was the Romans who brought taxation to the Knoll and with typical efficiency they would have ensured that it was collected either in kind or in coins.

The widespread use of coinage was a further effect of Roman control. Using

Romano-British pot

money to buy and sell goods and services was an essential feature of what had become a developed economy. Moreover, to some extent, Britain, and Brent Knoll, now belonged to an early version of the eurozone where trade and commerce were facilitated by having a common currency. Coins were already in use in the late Iron Age but during the Roman period they became an accepted method of payment across all sections of the population.

Occasionally, some of the more adventurous residents would have counted their coins and decided they had enough to go shopping in either of the nearest towns – Bath, known as Aquae Sulis, or Ilchester, known as Lindinis. The journey would have involved an overnight stay at an inn or, if funds did not permit, a night out in the open. Having arrived at their destination the country visitors would have walked along the main street and made their way to the market stalls in the forum.

Depending on how much they had to spend they would have returned home well satisfied with their expedition. In the food and drink line they may have bought some unusual vegetables and herbs, some olive oil or an amphora of wine imported from France. Much as they may have been tempted by other more exotic fayre on display, such as lobster or peacock, it would have been too expensive to consider. Equally beyond their means were luxury goods like jewellery or silks but affordable household items like pots and knives could well have been purchased. Shopping, like taxation, had come to the Knoll and, except for the period after the Romans left, neither would ever disappear.

The first visit to a Roman town must have been an overwhelming experience for those who lived in the country. People had heard about towns but to walk their streets and gaze at their marvels was to enter a world of fantasy. They would never have seen anything like it before: rows of large houses, paved streets, fountains and statues, and great stone buildings with pillars and facades.

Buildings were different and so were the people. As well as wearing strange clothes their general appearance was unfamiliar. Depending on the fashion of the day men had short hair and were clean-shaven while women had elaborate hairstyles and wore make-up. Some people spoke a different language and some could be seen making marks on wax tablets. Anyone curious enough to ask what they were doing would have been introduced to a new concept in communication – the written word, which for the Romans was as important as the spoken word.

Visitors to Bath would have glimpsed the magnificent bathing facilities that can still be seen today. The baths represented the height of Roman civilisation both in the whole idea of public bathing and in the construction of the building. Close to the baths was the temple of Sulis Minerva built in the first century AD and subsequently enlarged. With its steps, columns and richly decorated stonework the temple precinct was a wonder to behold.

Broadly speaking native Britons would have understood the use to which the temple was put although they had their own beliefs about gods and spirits. Long before the occupation there were sacred places such as groves and springs where people would commune with beings from other realms. These rituals continued in Roman times when it seems that native and imported beliefs began to merge.

Temples were built in rural as well as urban areas with many being located on prominent hilltops. Excavations have revealed their presence at Henley Wood in Yatton and at Brean Down. Given that hilltops were commonly used as sites for stone built temples and given what was discovered by the Reverend Skinner it is likely that a temple existed on top of the Knoll. The building would have looked impressive and consisted of a central tower-like structure, the cella, which was surrounded by an ambulatory. Inside the cella was a statue of the particular god or goddess whose powers were to be invoked. One can surmise that the temple was used not just by the person who built it but by ordinary folk who had their own sacred places but were not averse to tapping into any other divine powers that were available.

The temple, the villa and the Roman coins indicate that the inhabitants of the Knoll did not live in splendid rural isolation far removed from what was happening in the rest of the country. Their day-to-day lives may have changed little but the effect of the Roman occupation was ever-present. Local people obeyed Roman law, paid Roman taxes, worked at a Roman villa, communed with their God at a Roman temple and used coins stamped with the heads of Roman emperors.

Fragments of pottery found on the Knoll

Saxons and Vikings

Roman rule came to an end early in the fifth century when a revolt by the British led to the expulsion of the administration. Life on the Knoll went on as normal but with an added bonus: there was less tax to pay as there was no army and no bureaucracy to support.

The country was not left on its own for long since next to arrive were the Anglo-Saxons. An interesting debate about this period concerns the actual number of invaders and settlers who came over. It used to be thought that a mass migration of Anglo-Saxons drove out many of the native British who found themselves pushed ever westwards to Wales and Cornwall. More recent interpretations of the period consider this to be unlikely and favour the theory that considerably smaller numbers of migrant settlers were involved.

Whether the numbers were large or small it seems reasonable to assume that protracted and organised hostilities took place between the British and the groups of Anglo-Saxons who did arrive. It is highly improbable that heavily armed warriors intent on seizing other people's land would have been welcomed with open arms. Gildas, the earliest chronicler of these events, was prone to exaggeration but by and large he was reflecting the realities of the situation when he wrote about dead bodies in the street, gleaming swords and crackling flames.

At this point we must refer to King Arthur again because it is from the mists of these uncertain times that his shadowy figure emerges. The question to which everyone inevitably returns is whether there was a real person behind the legend. Was there ever a king called Arthur, or indeed a king with another name, who led the Britons against the Saxons, defeated them in one major battle but finally lost out to them? Was there a charismatic leader who organised effective resistance against the invaders and around whom later legends grew? We do not know but it is at least a possibility.

Something we do know is that South Cadbury hillfort, claimed by some to be King Arthur's Camelot, was extensively refortified at this time. Whether this or other hillforts in the area were being used as a defence against Anglo-Saxon incursions is uncertain, but it must be possible that fighting occurred on some of them, including Brent Knoll. Nor is it totally fanciful to suggest that local men may have fought further afield under an inspirational figure who later became the template for the legendary Arthur.

When the Saxons eventually prevailed I doubt if the people who were living on and around the Knoll decided to load up their carts and make their

Viking longship with its distinctive sail, shields and figurehead. Raids along the Bristol Channel are recorded in the Anglo-Saxon Chronicle.

escape deeper into the south-west or over to Wales. They may have done, of course, and there may have been a wholesale take-over by a Saxon chieftain and his followers, but it is more likely that most of them stayed where they were.

They accepted a new authority and paid their dues in kind. They had different laws to follow, which in time were formally set down, and at some stage the community became fully integrated into the Anglo-Saxon kingdom of Wessex. Gradually the style of houses changed and different fashions in clothing began to appear. Christianity became the established religion and later on a small wooden church might have been erected by the local thegn as a place of worship.

One of the most significant changes that took place must have been in the language that was spoken. If the inhabitants of this area were mainly British they would not have been speaking Anglo-Saxon so how did they learn to speak the language which ultimately evolved into the English we speak today? One simple explanation is that it was necessary for the British to communicate with their Saxon masters in their language and therefore had to learn how to speak it.

Although certain aspects of life were not the same there was no change to the importance of farming on the Knoll. The land had to be farmed or there would have been nothing to eat. Fields were still ploughed, crops were harvested and sheep and cattle grazed on the hill.

It is on the slopes of the hill that we can complete the sketch of this period. The Knoll, as we have seen, can claim an association with a legendary king, but it can equally claim an association with a real king – King Alfred, or Alfred the Great as he is deservedly called. Most people know the story of how he burned the cakes while taking refuge on the Isle of Athelney but there is another charming tale about him which is less well-known. It is taken from his childhood and is found in a contemporary biography written by a Welsh monk named Asser who later became Bishop of Sherborne. One day, so the story goes, Alfred's mother was showing the young boy and his brothers a book that contained a long poem with a beautifully illuminated initial letter. She told her sons that she would give the book to whoever learned the poem most quickly. Alfred, enchanted by the illuminated letter, took it away with him and with the help of his teacher soon learned the whole poem which he duly recited to his mother, thus gaining his reward.

Describing Brent Knoll in his History of Somerset published in 1791 the Reverend John Collinson writes that King Alfred is supposed to have defended himself against the Danes at this "important fortress". He goes on to say that a "piece of ground southward of the hill preserves the memory of some notable skirmish in the name of Battleborough".

Although it adds colour to the local scene we cannot be completely confident that a "notable skirmish" ever happened. What we can be sure about, though, is that Alfred was not far away and nor was the Danish army. It has to be possible, therefore, that there was an encounter between the Saxons and Danes on the slopes of the Knoll even if Alfred was not personally involved.

There is an even greater possibility that skirmishes took place around the hillfort before and after Alfred's reign. Viking raids along the Bristol Channel are recorded in the Anglo-Saxon Chronicle before Alfred became king including in the year 845 when men from Somerset and Dorset fought against a Danish raiding-army at the mouth of the River Parrett and "took the victory". Attacks continued after his death and according to the Chronicle the islands of Flat Holm and Steep Holm in the Bristol Channel were used by the raiders as a temporary refuge. Local people certainly knew all about the Vikings and there were surely occasions when they came to know them at very close quarters indeed.

That these were undoubtedly turbulent times is reflected in the litany of slaughter described in the Anglo-Saxon Chronicle. For most people, most of the time, life carried on as usual but when raids did occur they must have been terrifying. The sight of approaching longships with their alarming figureheads and rows of shields would have brought fear and foreboding to any onlooker. Once in a while, I'm sure, square sails would have been seen from the Knoll as longships sailed menacingly up the channel.

Just as menacing for those looking across a different stretch of water at the end of this period were longships carrying warriors of another ilk. They were well-armed, well-disciplined and led by someone not interested in raiding but intent on the more serious business of claiming a throne. The year is 1066 and the Normans are about to enter the story of the Knoll.

5

THE MIDDLE AGES

The Domesday scene

It is unlikely that news of the conquest would have been greeted with any enthusiasm on the Knoll. Judging by the hostility the Normans encountered elsewhere in the country the opposite was probably the case. Such was the resistance to the invasion it took at least five years for William the Conqueror and his small but effective army to establish control.

From the time of William 1 onwards we begin to know a lot more about Brent Knoll and the surrounding area. As a matter of course an increasing

Norman arch at Brent Knoll Church

number of written records relating to legal matters and the management of estates were being kept. In the stillness of monasteries in particular, monks assiduously compiled detailed information about monastic estates and many of these records have survived. It is from the documents produced by the monks at Glastonbury that we can see, for example, the precise crops that were grown here, the animals that were kept and the sort of work the villagers were required to do.

But the greatest written record of the period, one of the greatest ever, was the Domesday Book. It is an extraordinary document which carries us back in time – just as standing on the hillfort can do. To look at the entries in Domesday is to visit communities of almost a thousand years ago and gain a remarkable insight into what people did and how they lived. And, more than that, we can even read the names of some of these people.

In becoming King of England William 1 claimed ownership of all the land in the country which made the Domesday survey, in effect, an audit of his property to enable his dues to be calculated. It seems the information in the survey was not collected by officials riding from village to village questionnaires in hand as we might expect, but that instead the shire court was used as the forum for gathering and checking evidence. According to one estimate over 60,000 witnesses were probably heard during the course of the inquiry, a figure that confirms the enormity of the exercise. Sometime in 1086 one small group of these witnesses would have travelled from the Knoll to the shire court to present their testimony and it was from this, along with other information, that the Domesday entry for the area was made.

The entry takes its place among all the other entries that are found in what is called Great Domesday, the volume which covers most of the country. As well as Great Domesday, however, there is another text known as Exeter Domesday which relates to the shires of the South West. This was used as the basis for the main volume and contains more information including details of livestock. The translation below is from Great Domesday with this additional information inserted. It can be found in Volume 1 of the Victoria County History of Somerset.

> *The church itself holds Brentemerse. TRE. Alnod the Abbot held it and it paid geld for 20 hides. There is land for 30 ploughs. Of this land 4 hides are in demesne where are 8 ploughs and 5 serfs and there are 50 villeins and 47 bordars with 16 ploughs and 11 hides and 20 acres of meadow. There are 1*

riding-horse and 73 beasts and 60 swine and 82 sheep. To the abbot it is worth 50 pounds. And when he received it 15 pounds.

Of these 20 hides Roger de Courcelles holds of the abbot 1 hide. Ralph de Conteville holds 5 virgates. Alfric son of Euerwacre holds 5 virgates. Godwin the priest holds 1½ hides. They who held them of the abbot TRE could not be separated from the church. In demesne there are 4 ploughs with 1 serf and there are 3 villeins and 5 bordars and 10 cottars with 3 ploughs. There are 1 riding-horse and 9 beasts and 10 swine and 86 sheep. There are 5 acres of meadow and 6 acres of underwood. The value between them is 4 pounds and 10 shillings.

What does this entry tell us about the Knoll in 1086? It tells us an enormous amount but more importantly it conveys a vivid picture of life on the land, rich in detail and full of colour. We can see the picture without necessarily understanding all the terminology but a certain amount of explanation may be helpful.

Brentemerse, meaning Brent Marsh, refers to the manor of Brent which covered the Knoll, the villages of South and East Brent, land on the levels around, and also settlements at Lympsham and Berrow. We do not know what percentage of the total land was on the Knoll itself but we can safely say that ploughs were in use on its fields, it was where many of the animals referred to in the extract could be found and it was the place of work for a lot of the villeins, bordars and cottars.

The overall landholder was the church, more specifically the abbey at Glastonbury headed, in Edward the Confessor's time, by Alnod the Abbot – TRE is an abbreviation for "tempora regis Edwardis", meaning "in the time of King Edward". At the time of the Domesday survey Glastonbury was the richest monastery in the country and the manor of Brent was a valuable asset which had grown in value from 15 to 50 pounds since the Norman Conquest.

According to the entry geld was paid for 20 hides. The geld was a tax on land and the hide was a measurement of land, for the purpose of tax assessment, which varied in size but was generally about 120 acres. A virgate, the term used in the second part of the extract, was a quarter of a hide.

We are told there is land for 30 ploughs and in fact 31 are identified in the survey. Although in practice a plough team could consist of up to eight oxen and occasionally more, in Domesday it implied a standard team of eight. Land

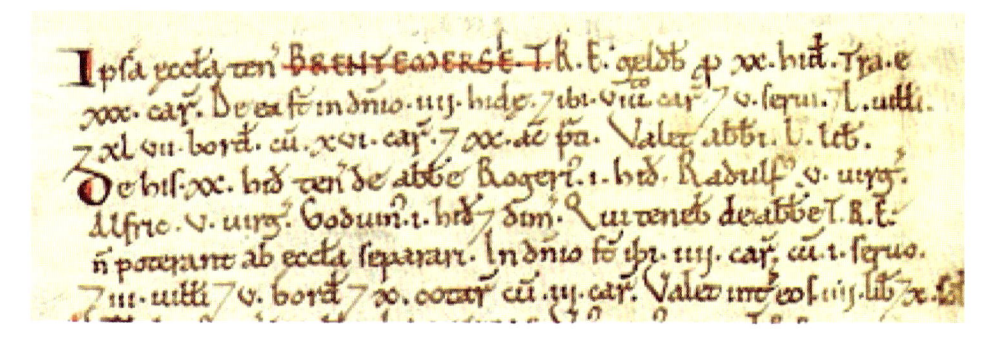

Brent Marsh entry in the Domesday Book

for one plough was an area that in theory could be ploughed by an eight-oxen team in a year.

Land in demesne was that which was farmed directly by the lord of the manor. Here in Brent the lord of the manor was the Abbot of Glastonbury and his demesne amounted to 4 hides served by 8 plough teams and 5 serfs. In addition to the serfs there were 50 villeins and 47 bordars employed on this land who also farmed their own plots amounting to 11 hides and 20 acres of meadow. Between them they had 16 plough teams to cultivate these plots on which they grew food for themselves.

As well as the Abbot's demesne there was other demesne land that belonged to the four major sub-tenants whose names are recorded. Their combined demesne was served by 4 plough teams and 1 serf, plus 3 villeins, 5 bordars and 10 cottars. These villagers had 3 plough teams of their own.

The villeins, bordars, cottars and serfs were the ordinary, anonymous but real people who populate the Domesday Book. Most prosperous among them were the villeins who had the largest amount of land, perhaps amounting to 30 or 40 acres, but who also had considerable labour obligations to their lord. At this time they were more free than the villeins we normally think of in the Middle Ages.

The bordars and cottars had smaller holdings or no holdings at all. Both groups owed service to their lord but because they only had a small amount of land their labour dues were less than those of the villeins. The serfs had no land of their own and were fully occupied in working on their lord's demesne.

Besides the ordinary people of Brent we meet those of higher status, the four sub-tenants of the Abbot of Glastonbury: Roger, Ralph, Alfric and Godwin. Roger de Courcelles and Ralph de Conteville were Normans who held land elsewhere, Roger with holdings in almost every hundred in the county. Neither of them probably lived in the area but they would have been interested enough in the management of their land to pay an occasional visit. Alfric was not a Norman knight but the son of an English thegn, Euerwacre, and Godwin the priest was also English. Both of them would have had their homes somewhere in the manor.

Along with the people we learn about their animals – the sheep, pigs, horses and beasts that once grazed on the Knoll itself and on the levels. The "beasts" were cattle, most of which would have been the oxen used for ploughing. It is worth noting that it was only the livestock belonging to the demesne that were recorded in the survey not the livestock kept by the villagers. If their animals had been included the total numbers would have been considerably more.

The Domesday Book has given us an enduring image of life in the manor of Brent in 1086. We see the folk who really lived and worked here and we can imagine how they led their lives. In its detail it was an ever-changing picture as different people came and went but on the whole the landscape of the Knoll and the lifestyle of its inhabitants remained constant throughout the Middle Ages. It was from this period that the villages on either side of the Knoll developed into more distinct settlements and gradually became the communities they are today.

Working the land

In the early Middle Ages the fields of the Knoll would have been more open and this would have been characteristic of the country as a whole. Many places had large open fields made up of long, narrow strips of ground that were cultivated by individual villagers or were part of the lord's demesne. Having long strips made ploughing easier as fewer turns were required by the plough teams. Strips held by villagers were not situated next to each other but were dispersed throughout the open fields so that everyone shared any differences in soil quality. Each field was planted with the same crop using a system of rotation which included land being left fallow for a year.

Here on the hill open fields covered the lower plateau while the steeper slopes and higher ground were mainly used for grazing sheep. The tithe map of 1842 shows the land on the plateau divided into narrow strips and it seems reasonable to believe that these had been here since medieval times. On the levels around the Knoll a lot of the land was pasture and meadow but,

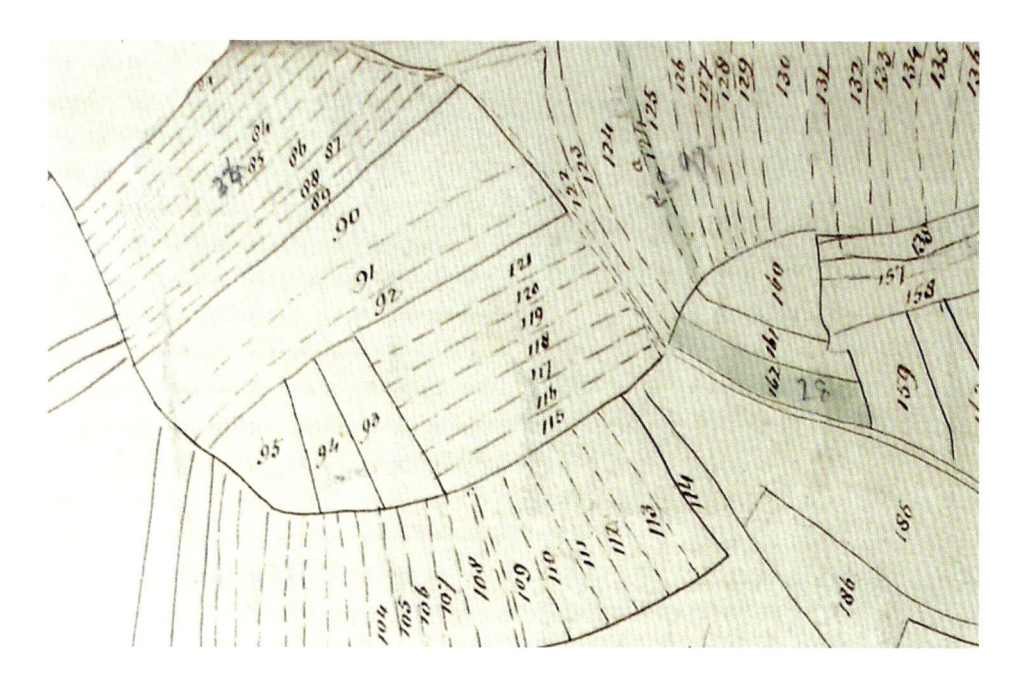

Section of 1842 South Brent tithe map showing the fields on the Knoll divided into narrow strips – see P61 for more of the map

surprising as it may seem, a substantial amount had been converted to arable by the Middle Ages.

Although the landscape was generally much more open it is likely there were a few enclosed fields belonging to the more prosperous members of the community as well as enclosed parcels of land close to people's homes where garden produce could be grown or livestock kept. Examples of the latter are the rectangular fields around the edge of the Knoll which would have had their origins in this period.

Apart from the landscape looking different from how it looks today, another difference would have been very apparent: there would have been people everywhere. The Knoll was alive with men, women and children either working in the fields or going to and from their place of work. Assisted by ox and horse it was human labour that worked the land and human labour that provided food for the table.

The villagers who laboured in the open fields on the plateau knew the meaning of hard work. Each day there was something to do and then, as now, farming was an all year round occupation. In winter livestock had to be looked after and fed, and as there was less to do in the fields this was the season for maintaining equipment and property.

Ploughing and sowing began in the spring and lasted into the autumn. Guiding the plough to produce a long, straight furrow was physically demanding requiring strength and skill throughout a working day that began at sunrise. Accompanying the ploughman was the ox-goader wielding a long stick with a metal point to persuade the team of oxen to keep pulling steadily.

At some stage after the plough came the harrow which was brought into action to prepare the soil for sowing. Long mallets called clodding beetles were also used to break up any large clods of earth. Grain seed was carried in a basket and broadcast as evenly as possible while beans and peas were carefully planted in the soil. No doubt after the fields were sown children from the villages came out with their slings to frighten away the crows. They would have enjoyed the sport but would not have been as accurate as their Iron Age predecessors who had used the weapon for a different purpose.

The rhythm of the seasons regulated the life of rural communities in the medieval period, exactly as it had for thousands of years previously and would continue to do for hundreds of years to come. After the hard work of spring, summer brought tasks of a different kind. It certainly did not bring thoughts of holidays or barbecues. June was the month for haymaking when the meadows around the Knoll would have seen great activity. Teams of men moved down the meadows cutting the grass close to the ground with their long-handled scythes. Women and children followed behind, turning the hay to ensure it dried evenly before being gathered into large stacks. A few weeks later cattle were put out to graze on the lush grass that kept growing.

Another essential task in the summer was shearing the sheep, the fleece being skilfully removed with hand shears. Sheep were valuable for small farmers and great landowners alike. They provided meat and cheese for villagers and townspeople. Their manure fertilised the soil and their skin could be made into a durable writing material. And, as if this were not enough, they also generously donated their wool for the benefit of humankind.

In medieval Britain wool was big business. Keeping sheep was common throughout the country and was often a well-organised and profitable enterprise. An indication of the scale of the wool economy can be seen in the enormous quantity of fleeces that were shipped abroad. Between 1304 and 1311 the annual average of wool exports was 39,500 sacks, each sack containing at least 250 fleeces. That amounts to approximately ten million sheep providing wool every year for the cloth-making industry of the continent. This was commerce on a vast scale and a trade in which the whole county of Somerset, including the inhabitants of the Knoll, successfully participated.

Sheep were a key factor in the prosperity of the area

Many of the sheep would have belonged to the Glastonbury Abbey estate or the larger sub-tenants but a sizeable number would have been owned by tenants with small amounts of land eager to have a share of the lucrative wool business. Some of the fleeces would have been kept by the villagers themselves for spinning and weaving at home in order to produce cloth that could be used for a variety of purposes. Other fleeces were taken to the nearby ports of Bridgwater and Bristol where they would be sold to the merchants who traded with Europe. It is quite possible, therefore, that in medieval

France or Italy people were wearing clothes woven from the wool of sheep that grazed on the Knoll – an interesting thought.

Not all the wool went for export. During the Middle Ages cloth was produced commercially in this country both for home consumption and for selling abroad. Over the centuries wool from the Knoll would have supplied the textile industry in the region, some of it probably being used in the making of Bridgwater cloth. Occasionally the fleeces that belonged to the Abbey may have been sent over to Glastonbury and sold with other fleeces collected from different parts of the estate. When that happened they would have been taken in a cart to Rooksbridge and loaded onto small boats carrying them to Glastonbury using a newly constructed waterway that we now call the Mark Yeo.

Harvest time followed the sheep shearing and in late summer nearly everyone was out in the corn fields from morning till evening. It was an impressive sight, and as with the haymaking, women and children could be seen working alongside the men. To harvest the ripe grain the reapers slowly advanced along the narrow fields of corn using a sickle to cut the wheat and a scythe to cut the oats and barley close to the ground. Following the reapers came the binders who tied the stalks into sheaves and put them in stooks ready to be carted away. Any residue of the crops left on the ground was too important to go to waste and was collected by those who did the gleaning.

After the grain harvest there were peas, beans and vetches to be gathered and more ploughing to be done before the new crop of wheat was sown. From the documents compiled by the medieval monks at Glastonbury we have detailed information about the crops that were grown here. In 1189, for example, the Abbot of Glastonbury, Henry de Soliaco, commissioned a survey of all his manors from which we learn that South Brent yielded the following amounts of grain and beans in cubic feet:

Wheat	Oats	Barley	Beans
3648	2106	490	1183

Later, in account rolls for the early fourteenth century, we can see the names of fields and the crops that were grown on them. I find it incredible that we have this wealth of detail from so long ago. One of the fields called Mill Furlong occupied part of the plateau close to where the waterworks are situated and in 1311/12 it was used to grow 20 acres of wheat. The name of the field suggests there was a windmill here and this would undoubtedly have been a good place to have one.

By November there was little left to do in the arable fields which meant that time could be spent on maintenance work. On the eleventh of the month the feast of Martinmas was celebrated and also used as the day when old livestock was slaughtered and salted to provide meat for the winter. It was getting close to the end of the year and Christmas would soon arrive. The villagers could have a holiday and look forward to some serious merrymaking and feasting and the possibility of an invitation to Christmas dinner at the manor.

Village life

The different tasks that accompanied the seasons convey a timeless picture of life on the Knoll and in thousands of other villages. It was a life that was led as close to the soil as it is possible to get and it was a life in harmony with the cycle of the natural world. Families were self-sufficient and farming was labour-intensive, far removed from the mechanised agricultural production we are familiar with in the twenty-first century. Looking back from our modern vantage point there are two ways of viewing the scene. On the one hand we can see the attraction of a simple life of honest toil where ploughs were pulled by oxen and seed was sown from a basket. On the other hand we

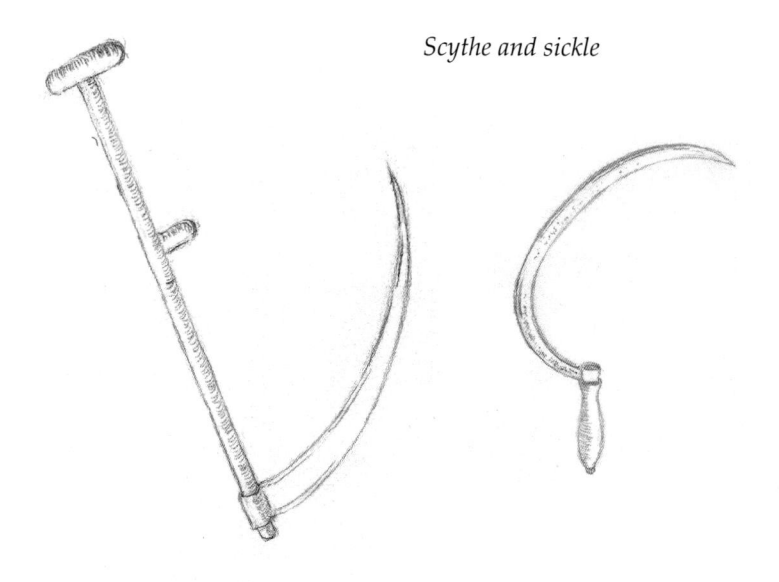

Scythe and sickle

can see the wind and the rain, the hard physical work and the long hours that were necessary in order for the villagers to cultivate their own fields and fulfil their obligations to the lord of the manor.

But our view is not how the farmers of the Knoll saw themselves. They would certainly not have felt they inhabited any sort of rural idyll but nor would they have been unduly concerned about the demands of their job. Hard work on the land was accepted as a way of life and without it there would be no food for the family and no home to live in.

Working hard for oneself was not something to worry about but labouring for somebody else was another matter. In return for the land they held as tenants, small farmers were required to work on their landlord's fields as well as perform other services such as carrying goods to nearby markets. I don't know whether the burden on local farmers in the Middle Ages was particularly excessive, or even whether they thought it was, but a survey of 1307 itemises their obligations. They included ploughing, reaping, carrying hay, ricking, threshing and transporting goods for the Abbot of Glastonbury, including his wine. In addition to these specific labour obligations there was "daywork" – the requirement to work one day a week in the service of the Abbot on other jobs like weeding, ditching or maintaining flood defences in the manor.

Having to provide labour for the Abbot was not the only burden to be borne by the villeins of the Knoll. There were manorial dues to be paid such as merchet, a payment on the marriage of a daughter, or heriot, a payment made on the death of a tenant often in the form of the best farm animal. On top of these manorial dues there were tithes to pay to the Church and sometimes taxes to pay to the King.

Given the demands on their labour, and the fruits of their labour, it would be surprising if those who worked on the Knoll did not have regular grievances against those at the upper end of the feudal pyramid. They were well aware that what was being taken from them in labour or in kind was not being returned to them in the form of services that benefited the whole community. Their payments were simply supporting the extravagant lifestyles of their wealthy masters.

But despite their burdens, despite worries about poor harvests and despite the hard, unremitting, physical work that had to be done, I don't see a downtrodden peasant class here on the Knoll or anywhere else in the manor of Brent. I don't see grinding poverty and helpless people producing just enough to subsist on. They had their bad days and their bad years, as we all do, but permanent misery – I don't think so.

Because the land and the climate were good the soil produced more than enough to live on. Surplus grain and livestock would have been traded with a view to making a small income and an entrepreneurial spirit would have been a feature of the local economy. Some people acquired more land to improve their prospects further and would thus have had the means to buy new farming equipment, household goods and maybe some of life's little luxuries. Carpenters, blacksmiths, thatchers and others who had set themselves up in specialist trades began to find an increasing demand for their services.

The villagers lived in what they considered to be comfortable homes although this is not how we would describe them since they lacked the amenities we take for granted. There was no proper sanitation, no running water, no electric lighting and no glass in the windows. The furniture was basic, to say the least, consisting of benches, stools, a table, storage chests, and beds that were mattresses stuffed with straw. But this was home, and what we would regard as discomfort was perfectly acceptable to our medieval forebears.

Most of the houses were well-built and of a good size. Many of them may have been as large as 15 ft by 45 ft with walls made from wattle and daub and thatched roofs supported by crucks. A fire was used for cooking and heating, and lighting was provided by rushes dipped in animal fat. Doors, with locks and keys, were hung on iron hinges, and shutters were made for the windows. Towards the end of the fifteenth century some of the houses may have had an upper floor.

People who worked on the land generally wore simple clothes with women dressed in long kirtles and surcoats and men in short tunics. Some clothes were made at home from wool spun by hand and woven into lengths of fabric, and some were made from cloth purchased at the markets in Axbridge or Bridgwater. Clean clothes were not put on every day but let's hope they were changed fairly regularly even if washing them by hand was time-consuming.

The families who lived here in the Middle Ages normally had enough to eat. They did not indulge in the lavish meals served up to someone like the Abbot of Glastonbury but they ate well and had a healthy diet. A lot of bread was consumed in the form of a course dark loaf made from a mixture of wheat and rye, or barley and rye, and there were regular meals from the cauldron of pottage that simmered over the fire in every household. The pottage contained a variety of nutritious ingredients: barley grains, or dried beans or peas, with onions, leeks and other vegetables grown in the garden, plus any meat that was available.

There was more to their diet, however, than bread and soup. The few cows and sheep owned by many of the villagers provided milk, butter and cheese and, along with the pigs that were kept, contributed to the supply of meat. Chickens were a constant source of eggs and made a tasty meal when turned on a spit over the fire. On the marshy, uncultivated areas of the levels there was extra food to be found just as there had been since prehistoric times.

Special treats like cakes and pastries were prepared on feast days. These were the holy days, from which our word holiday is derived, and they were indeed proper holidays. They were interspersed throughout the year and were an opportunity to have a break from work, indulge in a great deal of eating and drinking and enjoy sports and games like wrestling, archery or an early version of football.

Before the festivities began the villagers made their way to mass at one of the two great churches that stood on either side of the Knoll. By the late

Medieval bench end in Brent Knoll Church

Middle Ages these would have looked very similar on the outside to the way they are today, having been rebuilt and enlarged over the course of several centuries. Inside they had a different appearance, the walls being painted, for instruction more than decoration, with scenes from the Bible and pictures of the Last Judgement. There were now pews to sit on where previously people had stood, apparently not always with due reverence for the proceedings.

The Church played an important part in village life. Adult parishioners were expected to attend mass regularly and both churches on the Knoll were available for prayer and confessions. The feast days of the Church calendar enabled people to take time off work and enjoy themselves and the many saints that were remembered were on hand to provide support for every occasion: St Christopher when there was a journey to be made, St Appollonia if someone had toothache, and ominously, St Sebastian for protection against the plague.

The Church was present at births, marriages and the closing of lives. Baptisms took place in church immediately after a baby was born to ensure that in the event of early mortality it did not die in a state of original sin. Wedding vows were exchanged at the church door and were followed by a nuptial mass inside. At the ending of a life the priest came to administer the last rites, and for the funeral the body sewn in a shroud was carried into church on a bier draped with a black pall.

People with shared beliefs and traditions were brought together on a regular basis by the two churches which served the emerging villages and in this way religion strengthened the sense of community. And for the people working on the Knoll in the Middle Ages the local community mattered. It mattered because it enabled them to work with each other and, more importantly, to live with each other.

6

TUDORS TO TECHNOLOGY

Rooted in the soil

We think of the Middle Ages coming to an end when Henry VII became king after the Battle of Bosworth in 1485. There are good reasons for this date being chosen but, like similar dates, it was not a moment in time when society suddenly changed from one way of life to another. Most people continued to work on the land and what the land produced formed the basis of the economy. This was as true for Brent Knoll as it was for other rural areas.

In 1485 the manors of East and South Brent still belonged to Glastonbury Abbey, although not for much longer. With the dissolution of the monasteries under Henry VIII the Brent estate which had been in the possession of the Abbey since Saxon times acquired new owners. It briefly passed to the Duke of Somerset in 1547 and then on to a number of different lords of the manor.

From records kept by Abbot Beere in the early sixteenth century we can see that about a quarter of the land was arable and almost three-quarters meadow and pasture. We can also see detailed information about individual tenants and their holdings. In East Brent there were 91 and in South Brent 77. We are told their names and how much land they held and by having this information we can get to know who lived and worked here five hundred years ago. There was Walter Gynon, for example, who lived in East Brent. According to the survey he held "one messuage with curtilage, garden and orchard containing 3 perches and one croft annexed containing 1½ acres". He also held "18 acres and 1 perch of land, meadow and pasture enclosed" which included fields of 7 acres and 1½ acres on the east side of the Knoll. In addition to this he had 7 acres of arable, two of which were enclosed.

It is interesting to see how much of Walter's land was enclosed. He was not the only local farmer who by now held much of his land in fields with proper boundaries of hedges, ditches or fences. Later on, by the beginning of the seventeenth century, it seems that a lot of the Knoll and the surrounding levels had been enclosed although a fair amount of arable was still cultivated in open fields. On the lower plateau the arable strips remained as they were in the Middle Ages and were farmed in the traditional way.

In the Tudor period and the centuries that followed local farmers prospered, buying and selling land and trying out new methods in order to improve their returns. Cereal crops were important and sheep were kept for their wool and their meat but, as in many other parts of Somerset, it was keeping cows that became the most favoured activity. Although cattle had always been present in the manor of Brent during the Middle Ages more of them now began to appear on the lower slopes of the Knoll and in the fields on the levels. Beef and dairy cattle provided meat, milk, butter and cheese for local needs and for the growing markets of Bristol and Bridgwater. As was noted earlier Daniel Defoe was evidently impressed with the quality of the cattle he saw on his travels through Somerset and doubtless the quality locally would have matched that in the rest of the county.

Moving through the centuries we find two Enclosure Acts in the 1790s but these only applied to a small amount of land as there was little left to enclose. Of greater interest in terms of how the Knoll was looking it is necessary to study the tithe maps and tithe apportionments for the parishes of South and East Brent drawn up between 1840 and 1842. Like the Domesday Book and the medieval surveys they are a snapshot of history informing us about people as well as the land. Each plot of land marked on the maps has a number which corresponds to an entry in the record of apportionments. The entries are listed alphabetically under the landowners' names and show who occupied the land, how it was cultivated and its size in acres, roods and perches. In the final column the amount of rent payable to the vicar or rector is recorded.

These maps and apportionments are exciting and illuminating documents in which, once again, we encounter real people. There is a long list of them, owners and occupiers, and not only can we discover exactly the plots of land they owned or farmed we can see where they lived. Looking at the record for South Brent we come across Robert Good who lived on Burton Row and owned a house, garden and orchard extending to over two acres. Two doors away, in the direction of East Brent, William Harris owned and occupied a similar sized plot of land also with a house, garden and orchard but with a small copse as well.

South Brent tithe map, 1842

Both plots stretched up the slopes of the Knoll to the plateau, Robert Good's meeting the field known as Mill Furlong. This was one of the fields still divided into narrow strips and here we find, among others, James Frost occupying the strip marked 104 on the tithe map and Henry Cox occupying strip 105. We know the strips were arable but there is no information about what was grown on them. Some may have been used for cereal crops if adjacent owners cooperated with each other and some may have been used for growing potatoes or vegetables commercially.

Next to Mill Furlong was Brent Hill Field with more strips of arable land. We can see that here Mary Giles owned strip 119, farmed by William Body, and Sarah Martin owned strip 121, farmed by George Jervis. These are only a few examples but all over the Knoll and on the levels it is possible to see who owned and occupied the different fields, how large or small they were and how they were being cultivated. What stands out clearly in respect of South Brent as a whole is the fact that, overwhelmingly at this time, the land was given over to pasture and meadow rather than arable.

The fields on the levels were grazed mainly by cattle. On the Knoll itself there were cattle and sheep, as well as the arable on the plateau. In addition to the use of land for livestock and crops many people also had orchards that were often attached to their homes. A total of one hundred and thirteen orchards are recorded for South Brent which shows how important to the village they were. The fruit from the trees would have made sweet dishes and preserves and, of course, cider, the drink for which Somerset is renowned.

Dabinett apple used for cider that is still produced locally

For me the most telling feature of the tithe documents is the way they reveal the large number of people who had a stake in the land as recently as the middle of the nineteenth century. Away from the green fields of Somerset the great, unstoppable process of industrialisation was gathering momentum and creating large cities, factories, mass-produced goods and the comforts of modern life that today we take for granted. But here, around the Knoll, people were still rooted in the soil. Like factory workers they were engaged in production but it was food they were producing not manufactured goods. They continued to produce for themselves but more than ever before they produced for the growing population to be found in our towns and cities.

Self-sufficient communities

For thousands of years the land on the hill and the levels was central to people's lives. It provided employment and income for those who worked in farming and was the basis for the whole local economy.

Extract from South Brent tithe apportionment

The entries for South and East Brent in Kelly's Directory of 1861 reveal that the majority of named individuals are farmers but that alongside them is a wide range of other occupations: blacksmiths, wheelwrights, drapers, bakers and shoemakers to mention a few. It is clear that both villages were vibrant, self-sufficient communities easily capable of supplying their residents with most of their everyday needs. This essential characteristic of self-sufficiency would be preserved well into the twentieth century when car ownership and changing patterns of consumption gradually transformed the villagers' shopping habits.

The directory included the names of those who were involved in business and commerce along with the village notables. Not included were the residents at the lower end of the social scale, such as farm labourers, who did not share in the growing prosperity of the area. These were the men who toiled long hours for low wages in order to feed and clothe their families. For a complete picture of the inhabitants of the villages in 1861 it is therefore

Kelly's Directory for East Brent, 1861

Denison Venerable George Anthony, M.A. archdeacon of Taunton [vicar]
Goldsworthy Mr. John Andrew
Kent Mr. John
Millard James, esq
Norvill Miss
Purnell Mr. William

COMMERCIAL.

Allen John, draper & grocer
Arney Edward, farmer
Arney John, farmer
Baker John, tailor
Beacham John, butcher
Binning John, butcher
Board Robert, farmer
Bowley Elizabeth (Mrs.), *Wellington inn*
Burrows Thomas, farmer
Chapman Arthur, farmer
Churchill Charles, saddler
Collard Samuel, draper & grocer
Cook Arthur, draper & grocer
Cook Robert, farmer
Cook Thomas, farmer
Day James, bricklayer
Day John, farmer
Day Richard, farmer
Dibble Edward, farmer
Dibble George, farmer
Dibble George, farmer, North Yeo
Frost George Miles, *Brent Knoll inn*
Gane George, relieving officer
Haines Sarah (Mrs.), farmer
Hall Jesse & Edwin, carpenters & wheelwrights
Hatch Charles, shopkeeper & post receiver
Hawkins Francis, farmer
Higgs Elisha, farmer
Higgs George, assistant overseer
Higgs John, farmer
Higgs John Edwd. farmer & land agent
Hobbs Edwin, cattle dealer
Hodges —, grocer & draper
House Jonas, farmer
Hubbard Ann (Mrs.), blacksmith
Hudson John, farmer
Hudson Joseph, farmer
Huett Jesse, farmer
Isgar John, farmer
Kerton George, farmer
Kinglake Richard, baker
Major Thomas, shoemaker
Millard James, surgeon
Morgan Thomas, farmer
Norvill John, farmer
Parker Samuel, blacksmith
Popham William, carpenter
Radford Job, boot & shoe maker
Rich Charles, farmer
Rich Edmund, farmer
Salvidge Thomas, farmer
Slade George, farmer
Spriggs Thomas, cattle dealer
Venn William, farmer
Whitting Charles, farmer
Whitting George, farmer
Whitting Mary (Mrs.), farmer
Young Charles, butcher

POST OFFICE.—Charles Hatch, receiver. Letters from Weston arrive at 7.30 a.m., dispatched at 4.30 p.m. nearest money order office is at Highbridge

necessary to look at the census returns as well as the directories and these clearly show the large number of agricultural labourers who were employed here.

Although everybody was aware of their social status and observed the proprieties of their position, both villages would have retained the sense of community that had developed in the Middle Ages. Whether they were of high or low estate the residents belonged to a close-knit group of people who lived near each other and depended on each other. They shared an understanding of the countryside and an instinctive feel for farming and the land. They came together in church or chapel and when there was a time to celebrate or a time to mourn.

One communal celebration has a long tradition. People have been celebrating the successful harvesting of their crops since farming began and feasting and drinking have always been an important part of the celebrations. At East Brent a Harvest Home was inaugurated in 1857 by Archdeacon Denison and John Higgs, a churchwarden and farmer. It remains a popular annual event with lunch being served in a large marquee at the foot of the Knoll. Halfway through the meal a parade of ladies and children arrives carrying the puddings followed by four men bearing a large harvest loaf on their shoulders.

From the Tudor period down to modern times the villagers lived in a variety of accommodation. Labourers occupied small cottages while more affluent residents owned larger dwellings and began to take an interest in houses built of red brick. Inside people's homes furnishings varied according to income and prevailing fashion and the same applied to the widely different styles of clothing that would have been seen. For work and domestic duties most people wore simple clothes but the wealthier classes had extensive wardrobes that would have matched any of the period costumes which regularly catch our eye in television dramas.

Over the years there were fewer changes to people's diet than there were to their clothing. The food they ate stayed more or less the same until the twentieth century and nearly all of it was locally produced. Savoury dishes consisted of meat, fish, eggs, cheese and vegetables with home-grown potatoes also making an appearance. Fruit from the orchards was used for puddings and tarts, and jam-making became popular in many households.

Some things, of course, were not sourced from nearby farms. Tea, for example, was sipped in drawing rooms soon after it became a fashionable drink, and produce from warmer climates was consumed by those who could afford it well before it became widely available.

The community living around the Knoll was self-contained but never isolated. People found out what was happening in the wider world by meeting with traders at the markets, by talking to travellers or even by venturing further afield themselves. They knew about improved methods of house-building, or the latest fashion in clothing or any new food or drink that appeared on the scene. Sometimes rapidly, sometimes gradually, developments in society as a whole were taken up by the inhabitants of the two villages and invariably these brought improvements to the quality of their lives.

The effects of conflict

Unfortunately not everything imported from the outside world had a beneficial effect. One of the most undesirable of all imports to the area has been that of conflict. It came to the Knoll in the Iron Age, and afterwards when the Romans, Saxons and Vikings arrived. Less obviously, perhaps, its effects were felt during the Middle Ages when local men would have been involved in the wars against the Welsh, the Scots and the French.

The clouds of war continued to hang over the Knoll in every century after the Middle Ages. We have already looked at the confrontation between Queen Elizabeth I and Phillip II of Spain when for a long time the villagers played their part in preparing for an invasion. The muster rolls of 1569 show the names of the men who were enlisted in the militia well before the Armada set sail.

Tithing of Este Brinte.

ABLEMEN.

Heughe Bathe	... archer.	Richd. Lander	... archer.
Walt. Jones	... pekeman.	John Wingode	... pekeman.
John Adams	... „	Robt. Sime	... archer.
John Symons	... billman.	Wm. Pytte	... gonner.
Wm. Taler	... gonner.	John Nevell	... pekeman.

ARMOR.

i tithing corslet furnished.
i tithing peire of almon revitts furnished.
i Harquebut, ii bowes, ii sheifs of arrowes, furnished.
John Symons with others } one peire of almon revitts.

Muster roll for East Brent

In the following century civil war erupted and people living here found themselves caught up in events affecting the whole country. There were no battles or skirmishes in the vicinity but on one occasion there was an unsettling disturbance. In 1645 a troop of Royalist Cavalry quartered themselves on the loyal inhabitants of South Brent and, with no thoughts of gratitude, took the opportunity to plunder the village. People were threatened with violence and made to hand over money, horses and other items including, it seems, 3 lambs and a sheep from Willy Filtham and 12 bushels of malt from Steven Cocke. Not surprisingly this provoked the villagers into taking action and on 4th April 1645 they set upon the Royalist troops with justifiable ferocity resulting in a lieutenant being shot in the thigh.

The two ringleaders of the "tumult and insurrection", as it was referred to, were deemed to be John Somerset, a local gentleman, and a certain Thomas Gilling. They were both arrested and taken to Bristol jail where they were held for a number of weeks accused of inciting the riot. Whilst there they wrote a letter to their wives asking them to carry on with the "ploughing and husbandrie" as normal and to keep their spirits up by drinking a cup of sack, as they themselves were doing. The letter also asks John's wife, Joan, to present some partridges to the Governor of Bridgwater where the Prince of Wales, the future Charles II, happened to be staying at the time. It was evidently felt that this would be a timely gesture and helpful in securing their freedom if the Prince could be persuaded to intercede on their behalf.

Fortunately for John and Thomas, and to the relief of all concerned, they were not put on trial. Instead they were both released on bail in the sum of £500 and bound over to be of good behaviour. With the Royalists losing ground to the Parliamentary forces it was probably decided there was little to be gained from having supporters of the King locked up in jail. It would be no surprise if the two men's loyalty to the Royalist cause was somewhat diminished when they returned home and, mindful of their recent experience of the King's army, the same would have been true for most people.

The Civil War brought disruption in other ways, as it did across the country, but it was war in the twentieth century that had by far the greatest effect on the community. Daily life was not totally torn apart as it was in the towns and cities that endured regular air raids but, nevertheless, local people were deeply involved in both great wars.

During the Second World War they followed events by reading newspapers or by listening to the news on the wireless. Like everyone else in the country their food, clothing and fuel were rationed but they quickly learned to adjust to the shortages. Farmers in the area made an important contribution to the war effort by increasing their production and in this they were helped by their wives, women from the villages and any Land Girls who had been drafted in.

Families in the villages made their contribution by taking in evacuees. Entries in the logbook for Brent Knoll school record that on 14th June 1940 arrangements were made to welcome 34 evacuees from Dagenham and that two days later 14 arrived from Walthamstow. They assembled in the school with labels pinned to their clothing and were duly allocated to their new homes.

I expect that most children were homesick initially but soon became part of the family. Over fifty years later, recalling her time spent in East Brent, one former evacuee describes how happy she was in her family and how friendly the people in the village were. She remembers earning 6d a week cleaning the brass for a lady who lived in Church Street so she could go into Weston-super-Mare on a Saturday afternoon.

Another former evacuee who lived with a family in Brent Knoll recalls how she found it difficult to understand the father of the household because of his strong accent. There was obviously a clash of accents at the time because some children made fun of the way she spoke. One afternoon a week she went with other girls to learn cross stitch from the kindly Miss Fry who had a big house in the village. When she was older she took her first job at a shop in Weston but later moved to a factory at Highbridge making flares for the air force. Here she earned 27s 6d which was a lot better than her wage as a shop assistant.

I like to think that many of the young wartime visitors climbed to the top of the Knoll and played on its slopes. If they had done so they would have

One of the slit trenches

noticed slit trenches being dug around the hill by troops who were billeted locally. The trenches formed part of the Somerset coastal defences which in turn were part of the country's enormous defensive scheme that was put in place between 1940 and 1941 when invasion was threatened. It is difficult to assess how effective the Knoll's defences would have been in the event of an invasion but their presence must have boosted morale and reinforced the prevailing spirit of defiance and resolve. They were a tangible sign that the country was following Churchill's famous call to fight on the beaches, fight on the landing grounds and, for anyone based here, fight in the hills. Two and a half thousand years after the hillfort was built it is astonishing that the summit of Brent Knoll was once more being prepared for military action.

Whilst recognising all that was done on the home front we know that the greatest contribution to the war effort was made by those who saw active service. These were the people who experienced at first hand the full horror of war. In whatever capacity they served, and wherever in the world they confronted the enemy, the men from around the Knoll displayed the highest courage which we have a duty to honour. In both World Wars many of them made the supreme sacrifice. Their names are inscribed on the memorials in East Brent and Brent Knoll and we must always remember them.

Technology

If conflict has been one of the least desirable imports from the outside world technology has surely been one of the most desirable. We have enthusiastically embraced its wizardry in every aspect of our lives and it has become the emblem of the modern era. It thus seems appropriate to end this brief history of the Knoll by summarising its effects.

Technology in the form of machinery was slow to appear in the fields. Throughout the nineteenth century, and on some farms into the twentieth, corn and hay continued to be cut by hand in time-honoured fashion using sickles and scythes. Until well into the last century, too, ploughs were still being drawn by horses.

Among the new machinery available to farmers who could afford to buy it were horse-drawn mowers and reaping machines. Threshing also became mechanised and machines for this process were pulled by horse from farm to farm. Contractors were often employed to do the threshing and as well as taking their threshing machines they took portable steam engines to power them. These, too, had to be pulled by horse initially but were later replaced by steam traction engines that both provided the power and did the pulling. The arrival of one of these gleaming monsters would have caused great excitement as would standing close to one of them as it did its work.

More than anything else the piece of technology that transformed farming all over the world was the tractor. In this particular corner of the world it has served as a multi-purpose machine on the hill and on the levels. Although tractors had been in use since the early years of the twentieth century it was not until the Second World War that they became a more familiar sight in the fields of the Knoll.

It was always interesting to watch new farm machinery in action but nothing could beat watching a steam train thundering along the Great Western railway line. Here was technology that everyone could use and its benefits soon became apparent after the station at Brent Knoll opened in 1875.

Brent Knoll station

People could now travel anywhere in the country cheaply, conveniently and comfortably. Bridgwater, Weston and Bristol were within easy reach for shopping and before long it was possible to take a day trip further afield – to somewhere like Exmouth, perhaps.

There were other benefits apart from passenger travel. Goods of all shapes and sizes could be brought directly to the area as could national newspapers. Farmers were able to send fresh produce and livestock to various markets and milk was carried away every day to supply towns and cities like London, Bristol and Birmingham. The flourishing Cheddar Valley Dairy at Rooksbridge sent milk by rail to Cardiff and in the early days delivered it to Brent Knoll station by horse and cart in large seventeen gallon churns.

The last goods train to use the station was in 1963 and passenger trains stopped in 1971. By now the car was king and railways were in decline. Although I'm one of those who believe the car has been a hugely liberating invention that has enriched our lives immeasurably I'm prepared to concede it has had a number of adverse effects. One of these has been the building of major new roads through the countryside in order to reduce congestion and make journey times shorter. A few decades ago it was felt necessary to build a motorway with a route very close to the Knoll. Looking down from the hillfort this motorway is a spectacular sight and it serves us well, but every so often

Extract from Bradshaw's Guide, August 1887

we should remind ourselves that it has come with a cost, namely the disturbance to some precious rural tranquillity.

The coming of the car has undoubtedly brought many changes to the communities here and to communities everywhere. A change that is particularly noticeable has already been referred to: local shops have been forced to close partly because people can drive to nearby towns to do their shopping. At present, with the closure of a well-known butchers in East Brent, the post office and general stores at Brent Knoll is the only shop left in the two villages.

Technology always has a downside that has to be weighed against its benefits but overwhelmingly it has been good news. It is safe to say that the technological advances of the past hundred years have radically changed our everyday lives for the better. The supply of water, electricity and gas has brought unbelievable convenience and comfort to people living round the Knoll and, in their different ways, washing machines, microwaves, telephones, computers and dozens of other miracles of technology have greatly improved their lives, as they have the lives of all of us.

But some things do not change. The Knoll is still the same size and the same shape as it was when our hunter-gatherer looked out across the levels. There are still sheep and cows in the fields, and there are still people on both sides of the hill going about their daily business as they have done for thousands of years.

7

PLACES

A place to live

There is every likelihood that people have been living on and around the Knoll since the Old Stone Age. The reason why is obvious: it has always been a good place to make a home. For the earliest inhabitants there was fresh water available from the streams, a plentiful supply of food in the marshes and land that could be cleared and cultivated. Later on, when security became a factor, it was an ideal location for a settlement that could easily be defended.

For thousands of years generation has succeeded generation in the communities that developed here. Families needing homes occupied those that belonged to their parents or moved into other properties or built new dwellings for themselves. As different ideas were introduced about domestic accommodation, and as people became more prosperous, the design and construction of homes gradually changed. Here as elsewhere the most significant change was in building materials with stone and brick replacing wattle and daub.

The legacy of house building in the area is two villages of great charm and distinct character. East Brent is a compact settlement on one side of the hill and on the other side lies Brent Knoll with its long main street. Walking round the villages it is worth reminding oneself that every house is full of history, not so much in terms of how the house was built but in the daily lives of the people who lived there – the jobs they did, the food they ate, the clothes they wore and the good and bad times they had. Some of their lives will have been as dramatic in their own way as those of well-known historical figures.

Among the varied and interesting houses are a number of handsome properties, often built of brick. I can't help thinking of gracious living in a bygone era when I stand in front of them. What I see are finely dressed young ladies sitting in well-furnished drawing-rooms engaged in animated conversation about the fortunes of their neighbours and the eligibility, or

The Red Cow, Brent Knoll

otherwise, of the local young gentlemen. Visitors come and go on horseback and occasionally a horse-drawn carriage pulls up at the front door.

In the village of Brent Knoll brick built houses are especially noticeable. During the eighteenth and nineteenth centuries brick became a widely used material for house construction in the country generally partly because it was the fashion and partly because it was easier and cheaper than building with quarried stone. We cannot be certain where the bricks for the older properties were made but later on, for the most part, it is likely they came from brickworks in Highbridge, Burnham or Bridgwater.

The bricks have mellowed over the years adding to the attraction of individual homes and the area as a whole. I know of one project where the homeowners were determined to reuse the bricks that had formed some of the walls in the house they were rebuilding. The old mortar was chipped off each individual brick to enable it to be used again. There were a lot of bricks to get through but the end result was a splendid restoration which more than justified the work involved.

Some of the farmhouses in the villages were built of brick but some were built of stone. The names of a number of them have been preserved on what are now modernised homes. Apart from the farms there were other properties where a trade or business was carried on and this meant that for the blacksmith, the saddler, the shopkeeper and anyone else who had their own business, the house in which they lived served the dual purpose of home and work.

A place to worship

Places of worship have existed on the Knoll for over two thousand years. During the Iron Age there were special places like groves and springs where people could communicate with their gods and in the Roman period a stone temple probably stood on the summit. Later, when Christianity became the established religion under the Saxons, a small wooden church would have been built somewhere in the vicinity, possibly on the site of one of the two medieval churches that are still here today. For hundreds of years these fine churches have been great centres of Christian worship and an integral part of people's lives. They are used regularly as are the two Methodist chapels.

East Brent Methodist Church

St Mary's Church, East Brent

All four buildings are rich in interest and we will visit each in turn. Next to the traffic lights in East Brent is the small Methodist chapel where every Sunday a loyal congregation maintains the tradition of worship. I've always been attracted to the building's simple design – it has a solid but inviting look about it. Inside it is much more spacious than you might expect and is able to accommodate the larger congregations that attend on special occasions. One of these is the annual candlelit carol service where carols are sung as candles flicker among the neatly arranged evergreens.

As you drive into the village of East Brent from the main road the tall spire of St Mary's Church points to the sky straight ahead of you. This is a beautiful church which demands a few moments of silence in order to appreciate the amazing craftsmanship that went into building it. Shaping every stone by hand the medieval masons who worked here have left us a legacy that will long remain a source of wonder.

When you open the fifteenth century door you immediately become aware of the tranquillity that is present in all old churches. There are many interesting features to observe including a wooden gallery, a superbly carved pulpit and a stained glass window in vibrant colours that depicts the story of Jesus' arrest, crucifixion and ascension. One of the chancel windows is an exquisite memorial to a former vicar of East Brent, Prebendary Archdale Wickham. Its design celebrates his twin passions for cricket and natural history and contains delightful illustrations of both: birds and butterflies, and a picture of three stumps, a ball and a wicket-keeping glove reflecting the fact that he kept wicket for Somerset between 1891 and 1907.

Not seen by the church bells which sound as they ring and up the Knoll. have been ringing One was cast in Chamberlain of other ten years later Bristol. casual visitor are the make a wonderful out across the village The two oldest bells out for a long time. about 1440 by W London and the by a foundry in

Brent Knoll's situated on the left-Street about half a off the Berrow has a distinctive welcoming. Within being opened the so large that a constructed to take Methodist Church is hand side of Brent mile after you turn Road. Built in 1837 it feel and looks most a few months of congregations were gallery had to be more people. We can

Archdale Wickham's window

be sure that inside this charming building many a rousing sermon has been preached and many a Charles Wesley hymn has been sung with great gusto.

It was Charles' older brother John who climbed the Knoll in 1769 and declared in his journal that there could hardly be a more pleasing scene. Ten years later he returned to Brent Knoll to preach and did so again in each of the following three years. His deep Christian faith gave him the energy and resolve to carry out his punishing schedule of preaching and establish the Methodist Church for the nation and, ultimately, the world.

Brent Knoll Church is best approached by turning into Church Lane opposite the school. This way you have a view of the former vicarage and church sitting easily together although built hundreds of years apart in different materials. The size of this vicarage and the one in East Brent is a

St Michael's Church, Brent Knoll

reminder that in an earlier age the lifestyle of the rural clergy was, to say the least, comfortable.

Walking up the lane you reach the church which stands proudly in an elevated position on the slopes of the Knoll itself. At the front is the original medieval structure dating from the early fourteenth century and consisting of the porch, the vestry and the south wall of the nave. The impressive tower was added later and around the top of it some gargoyles can be seen. The back of the church, the north aisle, was erected in the late fifteenth century using a warm, pink-coloured stone and with its buttresses, balustrades and pinnacles it contrasts pleasantly with the earlier construction.

Entering the church through the south door the characteristic zigzag pattern of the arch is evidence of an earlier Norman building. Once inside there is much to admire. Below the fine wagon roof of the nave is a row of fourteen stone heads representing various medieval characters including a king with a forked beard and two hands grasping his crown. The north aisle has a magnificent carved roof divided into six sections which are further divided into sixteen. If you look closely you can see that each of the resulting ninety-six panels has a different design.

This roof is the work of great craftsmen as is everything else: the stonework, the pulpit, the John Somerset memorial and, of course, the bench ends. Simply using the skills of hand and eye, stone masons, carpenters and wood carvers took pride in making things that were both functional and decorative.

John Somerset memorial

The John Somerset memorial is full of detail and needs to be lingered over. We heard about John in the previous chapter and here we come face to face with him. Carved in plaster his brightly-coloured monument is a spectacular feature with a wealth of interest. On either side of John are his two wives: Joan, on the left, with her large hat and laced coif, and on the right his second wife dressed more soberly. John Somerset himself is a striking figure wearing the typically flamboyant attire of a Royalist in the seventeenth century. His sword and the military motifs around the portrait reflect the fact that for a short time he was captain of a troop of horse in the Royalist cause.

Equally full of detail and deserving close study are the bench ends for which St Michael's Church is renowned. Some of them date from the fifteenth century and among these are a winged calf or ox, representing St Luke, an eagle with a book in its claws and a scroll on its wing, representing St John, and two of a pelican feeding her young with her own blood – the "Pelican in her Piety".

The three bench ends that are most well-known may have been carved even earlier. They tell a cautionary tale. The main panel of the first bench end in the series, nearest the front of the church, shows a fox in the clothing of a bishop or abbot. He is addressing a gathering of birds and geese that together symbolise the ordinary people of this or any parish. Above the panel is a chained ape holding a money bag and below are two apes turning a pig on a spit. The money bag may represent the tithes that the parishioners had to pay and the roast pig the overindulgent lifestyles of powerful clerics. In the second bench end the fox, stripped of his robes of office, is brought to trial in front of an audience of geese and is then put in the stocks. Finally, in the third carving, the fox is hung by the geese and is about to be thrown to the dogs below.

A few minutes are needed to look at the bench ends in order to do them justice. They are truly extraordinary. A leaflet about them is available in the church but a more detailed explanation of their meaning can be found in the outstanding guide to St Michael's written by John Page. It not only contains scholarly interpretations of the bench ends but describes and interprets every aspect of this glorious place of worship.

Detail from one of the bench ends

However uplifting it may be, a special building is not an essential requirement for the expression of religious belief. People can come together and worship anywhere and where better than on the Knoll itself. Each year at Easter a service is held next to three large crosses erected on top of the hill.

Crosses on the Knoll at Easter

The crosses are visible from the roads below and proclaim the Christian faith simply and boldly to all who see them.

A place to learn

There has always been a close association between the Christian faith and education. In the Middle Ages the priests in the two villages would have provided some basic education for those who wanted it but it was in the nineteenth century that the Church began to build schools for large numbers of children. This was done through what was called the National Society. In 1841 a school was built next to the church in East Brent and twenty years later one was built in Brent Knoll.

Archdeacon Denison, rector of East Brent from 1845 to 1896, had strong views about the role of the Church in education. Under no circumstances would he admit children to school without insisting that they learn the catechism and attend church on Sundays. Given the strong Nonconformist presence in the village many parents no doubt felt aggrieved by his uncompromising position. In 1879, however, the situation changed when a new school was built in East Brent. Since this was not a church school, but what was called a British school, it enabled parents to choose where their children should be educated. The school building is now in use as the village hall.

Apart from differences in religious instruction, a subject given a high priority, the lessons in all three schools were broadly similar. Reading, writing and arithmetic occupied most of the timetable but space was found for some geography, history, nature study and needlework. Rote learning was the order of the day, along with blackboards and plenty of chalk. We do not know how strict the teachers were, and they were not all as severe as we usually imagine, but children were expected to obey their teacher and sit in silence unless they were answering a question or reciting out loud. For serious misbehaviour a leather strap or cane was available to punish the offender.

Pupils sat in pairs at wooden desks that faced the front. Younger children wrote on slates but older pupils practised writing in a copybook using a pen dipped into an ink-well. The nib pen and the ink-well were to remain well-used items in the classroom until the second half of the twentieth century.

School logbooks tell us a lot about schools in the past. They are not a record of everyday life in the classroom but as you read them you are drawn into a different era. Attendance was often a big concern. In the logbook for the British school at East Brent average weekly attendance rates are entered regularly having been meticulously calculated to one decimal place: 77.1, 65.5 and even as low as 39.6 – the decimal being point six of a child! The reasons

Original church school at East Brent

for poor attendance are clear and these shed light on wider social issues. One reason was illness. In January and February 1890, when 86 pupils were on the books, an influenza epidemic brought attendance down to half the number it should have been. Other illnesses referred to are whooping cough, scarlatina and measles, all of which were easily transmitted.

A further reason for poor attendance was taking time off to help with traditional seasonal activities. One logbook entry states that "Many of the older scholars are engaged in haymaking" and this would not have been an unusual occurrence given that children had been helping in the fields since medieval times. Other tasks in which they assisted were gathering potatoes, not part of the farming scene in the Middle Ages, and picking apples and blackberries. My guess is that most children preferred this outdoor work to the work they did in school.

Perhaps the biggest factor in the level of absences was simply a feeling among some families that going to school was not important. On one occasion the headmaster observed wearily that it was difficult to effect an improvement in standards owing to the irregularity of the children's attendance. He followed this by stating that the school attendance officer was quite powerless in the village.

Poor attendance was not the only worry for the headmaster. Since 1862, when the system of Payment by Results was introduced, funding was dependent on the progress children were making. In 1887 the report of an inspector's visit was copied into the logbook and it was not exactly a glowing endorsement of the school. The inspector wrote this:

> The children are in good order, but their progress in the Elementary subjects is scarcely satisfactory. Reading was very poor in the lower Standards; Writing was fairly neat; Spelling and Arithmetic were weak. Singing was good, Needlework was fair. The Infants are orderly but they are not as far advanced in the Elementary subjects as they ought to be. They are very backward in Reading and their Writing is not at all good. A general improvement must be shewn next year, or a Merit Grant will not be recommended.
> My Lords will look for a more satisfactory Report as a condition of an unreduced Grant another year.

It is clear what the inspector wanted to see: more reading, writing and arithmetic – the 3 Rs, the subjects that mattered most. School for the children of the Knoll in Victorian times was not intended to be exciting or enjoyable as

> Feb 3 Average Attendance this week 58.3.—
> Many of the children are still suffering
> from measles and sore throats.
>
> 10. Many of the children are still suffering
> with sore throats. Average Attendance
> this week only 56.0—
>
> 17 The School was closed for Four days
> this week, owing to the severe Snow-
> storms and prevailing bad weather
>
> 24 On Tuesday morning before the children
> assembled a large piece of the Ceiling
> in School room fell down owing to the

Extract from East Brent British school logbook

it is today. Its purpose was to produce literate, numerate and Christian members of society. Within these limits it was probably quite successful and maybe not always as dreary and mechanical as is commonly supposed.

Outside the classroom lay abundant possibilities for enjoying the pleasures of childhood. On the hill and in the fields there were adventures to embark upon and stories to be played out. There were places to hide, dens to build and slopes to charge down. There was no wireless, television or computer to keep children inside and social networking was done face to face in the open air. The countryside was an enchanting environment in which to grow up and compared with the towns and cities of our rapidly industrialising nation it was paradise.

We cannot leave the subject of learning without mention of another school which was part of the life of East Brent for many years. In 1940 Rossholme independent girls' school moved from Weston-super-Mare to the vicarage at East Brent. It catered for boarding and day pupils and developed a reputation for sport and drama. Many of the girls who attended will have fond memories of their school days at Rossholme which every so often they are sure to bring to mind.

More places

From places of learning to places of relaxation. The area is well served by establishments that provide good food and drink and comfortable accommodation. On the A38 at the corner of the turning to Mark is the Fox and Goose public house with a travel lodge adjacent to it. There are other hostelries across the country called the Fox and Goose but this one probably took its name from the bench ends in Brent Knoll church. It was once a coaching inn and is marked on a map of 1822.

Further along the A38 are the Battleborough Grange Hotel, nestling below the Knoll, and Brent House Restaurant, a popular venue for eating out. The Brent Knoll Inn at East Brent is reached by turning off the A370 at the traffic lights. Ale and cider have been served here for at least a hundred and fifty years and, as the name suggests, the inn has a fine view of the Knoll.

The Woodlands Hotel is quietly situated a little way up Hill Lane in Brent Knoll. It accurately describes itself as being tucked away in the beautiful and mysterious Somerset landscape far from the bustle of everyday life. Finally in the list of places offering hospitality there is the Red Cow with its unmistakable sign and the warm red brick of its building. This well-known public house can be found in Brent Street.

Many pleasant drinks can be enjoyed at these premises but the most essential liquid for those who have lived here has been water. Nowadays it is supplied from Cheddar reservoir via the waterworks situated on the lower plateau. Previously it came from streams, springs and wells which have long been places of paramount importance. One Brent Knoll resident recalls her grandmother extolling the virtues of the spring water from the Knoll that was piped to her house. It had health-giving properties, she claimed, and was ideal for washing clothes and hair. The young granddaughter was not so enthusiastic. She had seen tadpoles and water-boatmen emerging from the tap in the kitchen and decided to give the water a wide berth.

Over in East Brent, at an earlier date, Archdeacon Denison had taken an interest in the springs and streams to be found on the Knoll. Concerned that the villagers were sometimes using contaminated water from ditches he devised a plan to bring them a clean supply straight from the side of the hill. A series of dams and reservoirs was constructed on the stream running not far from the school and the pure water that collected was piped to a tank in the village. It was an impressive scheme that would have brought an immediate improvement to the health of the inhabitants for which they would have been

Map of Denison's reservoirs *To face p. 405.*

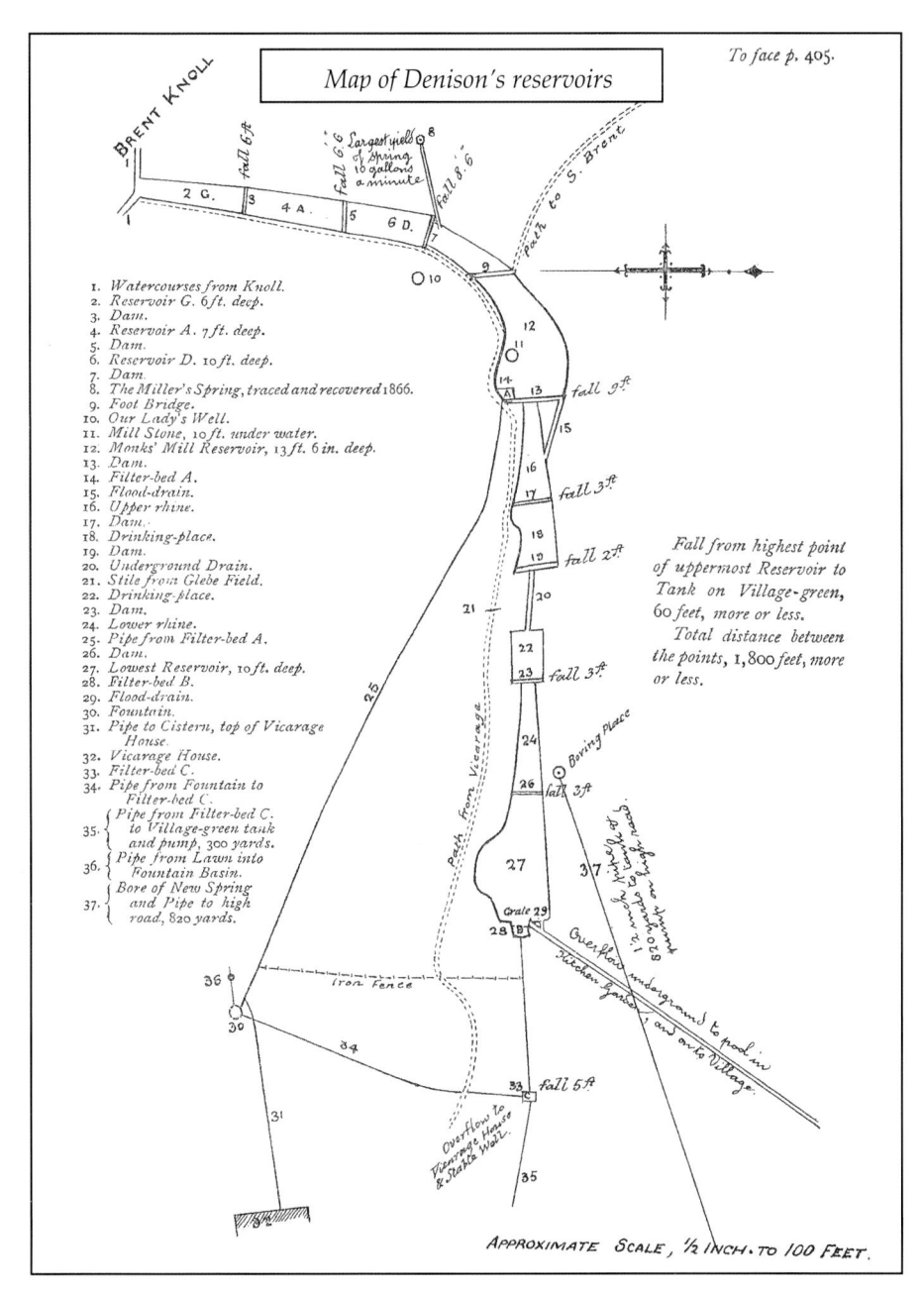

1. Watercourses from Knoll.
2. Reservoir G. 6 ft. deep.
3. Dam.
4. Reservoir A. 7 ft. deep.
5. Dam.
6. Reservoir D. 10 ft. deep.
7. Dam.
8. The Miller's Spring, traced and recovered 1866.
9. Foot Bridge.
10. Our Lady's Well.
11. Mill Stone, 10 ft. under water.
12. Monks' Mill Reservoir, 13 ft. 6 in. deep.
13. Dam.
14. Filter-bed A.
15. Flood-drain.
16. Upper rhine.
17. Dam.
18. Drinking-place.
19. Dam.
20. Underground Drain.
21. Stile from Glebe Field.
22. Drinking-place.
23. Dam.
24. Lower rhine.
25. Pipe from Filter-bed A.
26. Dam.
27. Lowest Reservoir, 10 ft. deep.
28. Filter-bed B.
29. Flood-drain.
30. Fountain.
31. Pipe to Cistern, top of Vicarage House.
32. Vicarage House.
33. Filter-bed C.
34. Pipe from Fountain to Filter-bed C.
35. { Pipe from Filter-bed C. to Village-green tank and pump, 300 yards.
36. { Pipe from Lawn into Fountain Basin.
37. { Bore of New Spring and Pipe to high road, 820 yards.

Fall from highest point of uppermost Reservoir to Tank on Village-green, 60 feet, more or less.

Total distance between the points, 1,800 feet, more or less.

APPROXIMATE SCALE, ½ INCH. TO 100 FEET.

extremely grateful. When the reservoirs were full they must have made a pleasing sight especially when they glinted in the sun.

While the work was being carried out the remains of what the Archdeacon believed to be a medieval water-mill were discovered and some years later a millstone was found. It is an interesting possibility that there was a water-mill but I'm not entirely convinced mainly because there is not a great volume of water. Whether water power was harnessed here or not, however, another natural resource was certainly available to provide useful energy. For hundreds of years it was wind power that turned the millstones and ground the corn.

With their mighty sails windmills would have been familiar features of the landscape and Denison's millstone could well have belonged to a windmill rather than a water-mill. It may have been the windmill that replaced the one that probably stood on the lower plateau in the Middle Ages. In Brent Knoll village a windmill was also operating close to Nightingale Farm and in East Brent two were recorded in Abbot Beere's sixteenth century survey. Being able to grind a large amount of corn using wind power was an important technological advance of great benefit to the local residents.

It does not matter that the windmills no longer exist. They are nevertheless places of interest with a story to tell, like all the other places on the Knoll. In the fullness of time more information will be revealed about some of them and new stories will emerge. A tower, for example, is shown on top of the hill on

Tower shown on enclosure map

an enclosure map but when was it built and what was it used for? And what more will be discovered here about the Iron Age hillfort, or about the Romans or Saxons or any period in history?

We will end the chapter by visiting two special places that have already been referred to: the war memorials. Brent Knoll's war memorial is in the churchyard and East Brent's is at the side of the main road but should be reached by turning off at the traffic lights and driving up the side road. On the memorials carved in stone are the names of men who had unbelievable stories to tell, but whose final stories could only be told by others. They are the heroes of the Knoll and we should reflect on their sacrifice and honour their memories.

War memorial, East Brent

8

A NATURAL PLACE

Habitats

The Knoll may not have the wild landscape or natural habitats of the Mendips, the Quantocks or Exmoor but it is still a great place to be out in the fresh air enjoying the natural world. It is a place to watch the trees swaying, to gaze at the clouds or to listen to the song of the birds.

The main habitats on the hill itself are the hedgerows, fields, woodland and grassland while on the levels the rhynes and railway ponds form additional habitats. All these sites are havens for plants and creatures where, despite appearances, the struggle for survival is far greater than any of the struggles the human inhabitants of the Knoll have been involved in.

One of the best ways to appreciate the natural world is to spend time observing the ordinary plants and creatures that too often we take for granted. If we are able to spend a few moments looking closely at a familiar tree or a common wild flower, or watching what the birds are doing, these ordinary, everyday sights will instantly become extraordinary. The natural world can be enjoyed without any expert knowledge but having a basic field guide to hand invariably adds interest to what is observed. For wild flowers I use a well-thumbed copy of a Collins guide illustrated by Marjorie Blamey.

Plants

Hedges are one of the true glories of our countryside and yet, because of their familiarity, we rarely pause to admire them

Cowslips

Wild garlic

properly. The Knoll and the levels are covered with hedges that retain their dual function of defining field boundaries and controlling livestock. Since fields in the area were being enclosed as long ago as the Middle Ages, it is likely that this is when some of the hedges were first planted. During this period, and subsequently, they not only served to define boundaries and control livestock they were also a useful source of timber and firewood.

The method of dating hedges by counting the number of shrub and tree species they contain in a ninety-foot length is no longer accepted as reliable but generally speaking those that are species rich will probably be older. There are many fine hedges on the Knoll of varying ages, some with a limited range of species and some with a wider range, and they are all of interest.

A number of different shrubs and trees make up the hedges on either side of Hill Lane, including hazel, hawthorn, blackthorn, dogwood, field maple and a species that has most definitely not disappeared from the countryside, the elm. There is a widespread belief that elms have been obliterated by Dutch Elm Disease, the fungal condition that spread throughout the country from the late 1960s onwards. This perception is both correct and incorrect. It is not the elm as a species that has disappeared but, in fact, the mature elm tree. Young plants are not affected since the bark beetle that carries the fungus only feeds on the bark of older trees. Long stretches of elm hedge, such as can be seen on Hill Lane, are thus able to survive while taller specimens of the tree will succumb to the disease.

There is an elm tree in the lane, however, that is over 25 feet high and so far it has managed to escape being infected. Although it may not survive for much longer it seems to be telling us that one day fully grown elms will be restored to the countryside.

Spring and autumn are the best times of the year to admire the hedges on the Knoll. In spring the white flowers of the blackthorn are followed by those of the hawthorn with their distinctive and powerful scent. In autumn both trees display their fruit, the hawthorn producing red berries on which birds and small mammals feed, and the blackthorn giving us sloes, dark blue berries that can be made into wine or added to gin.

A hedgerow coming to life with new growth is one of the most uplifting sights in spring. Not only is there the miracle of tiny leaves emerging in the hedge itself there is the lush growth below and all around. I'm always thrilled to see this and never tire of looking at a mass of cow parsley and the splash of colour made by the red campion. Primroses and bluebells make a welcome return and away from the hedgerow cowslips appear in the fields. The wild garlic announces its presence to our sense of smell and I'm continually fascinated by the curious form of the poisonous cuckoo pint with its spadix and spathe, and later on its orange-red berries. All these plants are common on the Knoll and we should make time to wonder at their splendour.

More flowers can be seen in the summer particularly on the grassy slopes just below the ramparts of the hillfort. They include birdsfoot trefoil, thyme, self-heal, scabious, salad burnet and the charmingly named lady's bedstraw. An unusual looking flower is the agrimony with its slender spike of small yellow flowers. The plant

Elderberries

Bryony berries

has long been used as a herbal remedy for various purposes including the treatment of wounds. Low down in the grass the tiny, delicate eyebright can be found and as its name suggests it was once used on the eyes. It is a beautiful flower, one of my favourites, and worth getting down on your hands and knees to take a close look at.

Don't ignore the dwarf and musk thistle as you walk the Knoll in the summer. They may be thistles but they are truly magnificent flowers. Find some wild roses to enjoy and look out for another of my favourite plants, the burdock. In summer you will see the purple flowerheads and in autumn the brown burs that attach themselves to clothing by means of their hooked bristles. But sticking onto clothes is not their purpose in life. Their aim is to become attached to passing animals which then unwittingly carry the seeds away from the parent plant – one of the ingenious methods of seed dispersal that nature has come up with.

Returning to how attractive the hedgerows are in autumn, they have an abundance of berries in addition to those of the hawthorn and blackthorn mentioned above. Among them are blackberries, the only berries we can eat as many are poisonous, some deadly. Once a common pursuit, picking blackberries, it seems, no longer has the appeal it formerly had and the days when children took time off school to go blackberry picking have long gone. Bunches of elderberries can also be seen and these, like the sloe, can be used to produce a homemade wine.

A variety of plants trail over the hedges. The flowers of the wild rose have by now become rose hips and they are joined by the red berries of the bryony – black bryony and white bryony, two unrelated species. In late autumn comes old man's beard with its fluffy "beards" of white plumes each with a seed to carry away in the wind. Its other name is traveller's joy and a joy to behold it undoubtedly is.

Even greater joys are the many trees that grow in the Knoll's hedgerows, fields and small areas of woodland. We can admire their size and shape, their strength and suppleness, and the changing colours of their apparel; we can touch their bark and listen to their whispering. Trees bring a lot of pleasure and they make good companions.

Ash is the most common tree growing on the Knoll. One very handsome specimen stands alone in the field next to the beech trees above Ball Copse Hall. With its black buds, unusual flowers and bunches of keys in autumn the ash tree has year-round interest and merits more than a passing glance. For

Ash tree

centuries its strong, flexible wood has been used in a range of products such as tools and implements, carts, weapons and furniture.

The beech trees referred to are in a private woodland but can be appreciated from the footpath that crosses the adjacent field. Mighty and majestic this tree graces our countryside in many ways, not least with the freshness of its leaves in spring and its golden glow in autumn. Also glowing at this time of year are the field maples that have grown to a good size and which, like the ash and sycamore, have winged seeds. Noticeable for a different reason are a number of crab apple trees with their miniature apples, not to be eaten raw but made into crab apple jelly. As for the oak I have only come across two trees growing naturally, one of them very old, but many oak saplings have been planted in Ralph's Wood next to Hill Lane.

Making up for the lack of mature oaks are plenty of horse chestnut trees. Being non-native to this country they may not be so popular with the purists but they are a great favourite with most people including myself. I know they only attract a small number of insects but other riches more than compensate for this shortcoming.

To children the horse chestnut is known as the conker tree and long may they have the excitement of collecting shiny conkers fresh from their cases. These are one of the great delights of nature – for adults as well as for children. In spring the trees have sticky buds to observe, emerging new leaves, and candles of white blossom. If you examine the twigs of the horse chestnut closely you will see leaf scars in the shape of a horseshoe, complete with nail marks, and whether or not this is the origin of the tree's name it is an interesting feature nevertheless.

We can't end this section on plant life without mentioning the reeds down on the levels. They wave their tassels in the rhynes and railway ponds that surround the Knoll and in the middle of winter their colour brings a warmth to the landscape. As you walk alongside the rhynes look out too for yellow flag and fleabane, the latter so called because when it was burned it was said to drive away fleas. It is a much more attractive flower than its name implies.

Horse chestnut bud and conker case

Creatures

Jackdaws at the top of the combe

Different plants create different habitats and these are the homes and territories for millions of creatures on the Knoll. We normally only notice a small number of them as they are mostly hidden by vegetation or are under the ground but a serious study would reveal their presence and their huge diversity.

The hedgerows are important wildlife reserves populated by all sorts of insects, birds and mammals. Individual plants within a hedge can be habitats in their own right. The bramble, for example, attracts shield bugs, butterflies, spiders and many birds which feed on the blackberries, and similarly the hawthorn provides food for a variety of birds and insects as well as for bank voles and woodmice. These are both common plants, and for that reason perhaps considered rather ordinary, but when you look at the wildlife they support, they perfectly exemplify the way in which the ordinary is actually often extraordinary.

On the Knoll, as elsewhere, the birds of the hedgerows and woodland are at their most active in spring when they are looking for mates, building nests and feeding their young. However, they are not very conspicuous as they dart in and out of their cover and the best way to see these small birds is to feed them in the garden. Their songs can be heard anywhere but the footpath behind Brent Knoll church makes a pleasant location especially in the early evening. The distinctive songs of the chaffinch, great tit, wren, robin and blackbird fill the air with a celestial sound that befits the setting.

Even more distinctive are the calls of rooks and jackdaws, the rooks with their caws and the jackdaws with their chaks. They are birds that ask to be noticed, not only because of their calls but also because of their aerobatics which are wonderful to watch as they fly round their nests or roosting sites. The jackdaws are the smaller birds with grey napes and a more hurried wing-beat and are often seen near church towers and cliff faces as well as among trees.

Just as compelling are the aerobatics performed by the swallows that visit the area. Once as I walked along a footpath in June a small group of them put on the most dazzling display for me, skimming at tremendous speed just a few inches above the ground and diving and swerving fearlessly. I'm filled with awe when I think about the incredible distance they fly in order to raise a new family in this little corner of Somerset.

The bird you will certainly want to see when you visit the Knoll is the buzzard. It is a common sight but is still essential viewing, possibly because it is a bird of prey and has an element of menace associated with it. High in the sky its black silhouette is unmistakable as it uses the thermals and air currents to soar and glide effortlessly over the countryside. If you are lucky enough to observe one at close range, maybe sitting on the branch of a tree, you will immediately realise how striking these creatures are.

Down from the Knoll on the levels are two large and beautiful birds: the swan and the heron. A pair of swans and their cygnets could be swimming along one of the rhynes or a heron could be standing motionless in a field. Grey and white with a black crest it stands tall, slim and elegant. Its long legs, long neck and long beak are not, though, designed for the purpose of looking elegant; they are designed to make it easier to acquire the next meal.

Sharing the freedom of the air with the birds are the butterflies. At different times of the year various species are evident including the peacock, orange tip, speckled wood, small tortoiseshell and common blue. I find the exquisite colouring of the orange tip especially enchanting and its appearance in spring adds further delight to the season. Only the males have the orange tips on their wings which act as a deterrent to potential predators.

Although there is far more visible activity in the air than on the ground the Knoll is populated by the usual mix of common mammals. The larger mammals are rabbits, foxes, badgers and hedgehogs and the smaller ones include mice, voles and shrews. They all build themselves comfortable homes, have varied diets and like every other living creature go about their business of bringing new life into the world.

Swans and cygnets in a rhyne

Ralph's Wood

To see one of the natural wonders of the Knoll you will need to visit Ralph's Wood in the autumn. In a sense it is not strictly a natural wonder as it has been deliberately planted with saplings and shrubs but its stunning autumn display of berries and leaves allows it to be described, without any doubt, as a wonder of nature.

The shrubs are mainly a selection of those that can be found growing in the wild and among them are dogwood, guelder rose and spindle. White berries and bright red stems distinguish the dogwood in the plantation from the more subdued, but equally attractive, native dogwood that grows in nearby hedgerows. The guelder rose looks glorious with its shiny red berries and blushing leaves, while rose hips and cotoneaster add to the symphony of colour.

Most delightful of all are the fruits of the spindle. These are pink, four-lobed capsules that split open to reveal the orange flesh round each of the seeds creating an eye-catching effect. A spindle tree in autumn is a marvellous sight and one I look forward to each year.

At the head of a ride looking down to the spire of East Brent Church and across to the Mendip Hills a simple stone memorial has been erected to Ralph Rich who planted the wood. Although Ralph died in 2005 at a relatively young age he has left an enduring legacy that will give pleasure to many people for a long, long time.

Guelder rose in Ralph's Wood

9

A HILL AND ITS PEOPLE

People of the Knoll

With its fields, hedges and trees, and its wild flowers, birds and butterflies, the Knoll is a place to which plants and creatures have been drawn. Long ago it was a place to which people were drawn in order to work the land but now they come to climb to the top of the hill and enjoy the views.

It is not only visitors who are attracted to the Knoll. People choose to live in the area and make their homes in one of the two villages that sit on either side of the hill. Both settlements are more than a collection of individual houses. They are genuine communities where the residents of all ages come together in many ways and for many purposes. You only have to look at the large number of village organisations to see the strength of community life.

The people who have lived here make the story of the Knoll: thousands and thousands of ordinary folk from the Stone Age to the Iron Age, through Roman, Saxon and medieval times, down to recent centuries. Most of them are unknown and anonymous but a surprising number are not. We know their names, where they lived, the work they did, their place in the community, their misdemeanours, their pleasures, their pains, their sacrifices. And whether or not they can be identified they have all been real people leading real lives in real history.

Anyone who has spent time researching their family tree will be familiar with the enormous variety of sources that contain information about people from the past. Some of the sources for this locality have already been referred to. They include the Domesday Book, medieval surveys of the manor of Brent, muster rolls, directories, tithe apportionments, census returns and the war memorials. Every name mentioned in these sources is someone who lived here and trod the slopes of the Knoll.

Owned by the National Trust the summit of the Knoll can be enjoyed by everyone

There are many more people to get to know by delving into numerous other archives. Among them are manorial court rolls, parish registers, old deeds, local newspapers and, at a personal level, the letters and photographs that have been kept in families. One of the most accessible ways of discovering something about the previous inhabitants is simply to read the inscriptions on their gravestones in the two churchyards.

Another approach to becoming acquainted with people who once lived here is to browse through the on-line catalogue of archives held at Somerset Record Office. Just by reading the summaries of certain documents we are instantly introduced to some of the characters who have long since left the stage. There is Thomas Long, for example, a tailor who on 10th December 1622 was questioned about how he came to possess three hats that did not belong to him. Or there is Alice Willmott who had an apron and a handkerchief stolen from her chamber in 1664 allegedly by a light-fingered knave from Bleadon. Or, with more serious consequences, there is Gartred Perby, a servant to Nathaniel Gilling of South Brent, who discloses on 18th March 1672 that she is with child by James Harris another servant in the same household.

99

A rather amusing record from the archives concerns George and William Pitter who were no doubt related to each other. In June 1751 George was convicted of swearing thirty profane oaths and William of swearing sixty. The actual words they used are not revealed which leaves one puzzling over what precisely they were and what were the circumstances that led to their utterance. I wonder, too, who was doing the counting and how this was done. Was it the next-door neighbour, perhaps, putting a tick against their names whenever they used a profanity and were there occasions when some of the swearing was done deliberately to annoy this person? Somewhere in the background there is a story to accompany the case that was brought before the Justice of the Peace.

Coming right up to date I have had the pleasure of looking at a different sort of archive – a collection of transcribed oral interviews about the past with some of Brent Knoll's residents. This rich historical record beautifully evokes a bygone age when the pony and trap and horse and cart were still the most common forms of transport. Reading the interviews I've come across memories of the village school: the hobnailed boots that were worn by the boys, the gardening on a Friday afternoon and the sandwiches of bread and dripping as there were no school meals. I've read about the shops including the tailors, the butchers, the two sweet shops and Dart's stores where during the war ration books were in regular use.

Working the land has been an enduring thread in the story of the Knoll

I've learned about the businesses: the blacksmiths, the garage, the corn mill, the coal merchants, the milk factories and the saddlers with its "wonderful smell of leather and dubbin". And, of course, I've seen how farming was central to the life of the village. How one resident helped do the milking before and after going to school for which he would be given a penny a cow. How a thirteen year old dairymaid used to get up at 5.30 in the morning to round up the cows on the Knoll and milk them by hand. How someone bought his first tractor in the 1930s and how haymaking was always a busy and thirsty time when farm workers could drink as much cider as they wanted and often did.

The recollections vividly convey the experiences of growing up in the village. So sharp and rapid are the images that reading the accounts is like watching a documentary. In front of one's eyes are youngsters swimming in the rhynes, collecting birds' eggs, trainspotting, going to the point-to-point races on the Knoll and memorably sharing the drama of the day a bomb fell on the skittle alley at the Red Cow. Packed with interesting and amusing anecdotes these memories bring to life a recent era but one which seems a world away from modern society.

I like the anecdote about the lady of the manor who had a Model T Ford car and a chauffeur. One day she visited the school where, on her arrival, the girls were asked to curtsy to her. At that point, in a daring act of rebellion, a girl called Elizabeth refused to follow the accepted social convention and defiantly said to her face: "If you will curtsy to me, I will then to you. You are no better than my own mother."

Quite right too. She had summed up the basic principle of human equality. In doing so she was standing up for the ordinary, hard-working people of the Knoll who for me are the central characters in the hill's story. We have encountered some of the great and the good like John Somerset and Archdeacon Denison but it is the typical villagers we should look up to. Whichever century they lived in, and whether we know their names or not, they worked hard, provided for themselves, raised families and woke up in the morning with an assortment of hopes and anxieties. Everyone who lives here today should be proud of the lifestyles and achievements of their predecessors.

The Knoll itself has ceased to play a big part in most people's everyday lives. It doesn't give them security as it did in the Iron Age and nor does it provide them with food as it did in medieval times. But it does give people the opportunity to go for a good walk, listen to the birdsong, admire the view and

*Archdeacon George Denison, a well
known local and national figure*

think about the past. For those who live here the presence of the Knoll gently and imperceptibly enriches their lives and makes this a wonderful place in which to have a home.

A hill most notable

The Knoll may stand on its own in the middle of a plain but it has never been isolated from the wider world. Its inhabitants have always traded with nearby settlements and, from as long ago as the Iron Age, they have been consumers of goods from other countries. They have also been part of the mainstream of British history where they have been caught up in the great events and social changes that have affected the whole nation.

The way in which the people of the Knoll have been both self-sufficient and connected to society as a whole has been a strong and lasting thread in the history of this area. It is one of many enduring threads that have been present in the community here and communities everywhere – threads such as people working the land, looking after families, defending territories, worshipping gods, living with neighbours and adapting to new ideas. These are the aspects of life that have bound people together and shaped the course of human history.

I hope I have shown that Brent Knoll is a hill that is notable for its history even if for long periods continuity has been more evident than change. With human endeavour at its core I find it a noble as well as a notable history.

I hope, too, I have shown that Brent Knoll is notable for many other things: for its places, for its plants and creatures, for its geology and for its magnificent views from the summit. Families will make their homes here long into the future. Visitors will keep visiting and millions of people will continue to be fascinated by the sight of this most notable of hills rising unexpectedly in front of them.

Brent Knoll from Crooked Lane

Sources and resources

Places

In addition to the places mentioned in the book that I know reasonably well these are some of the places I have visited in the past three years whilst doing the research:

Brent Knoll itself and along its footpaths
The levels immediately surrounding the Knoll and further away
The villages of Brent Knoll and East Brent
Brean Down
Bridgwater Bay
Kilve beach
Gold Corner and the Huntspill River
Shapwick Heath
Pillrow Wall Rhyne, Mark
Hillforts at Cadbury Hill (Congresbury), South Cadbury, Ham Hill, Danebury and Maiden Castle
Peat Moors Centre (now closed)
Cheddar Museum of Prehistory
North Somerset Museum, Weston-super-Mare
Museum of the Iron Age, Andover
Somerset Brick and Tile Museum, Bridgwater
Glastonbury Abbey

Books and booklets

Local area

Geology of the country around Weston-super-Mare (1983) *A Whittaker and G W Green*
Ordnance Survey Explorer Map 153
Brent Knoll, Archaeology in the National Trust, Somerset (1980) *D Thackray*
A Brief History of Brent Knoll for the Village School Children, *Alan Oliver*
The History of East Brent, *E Yeoman*
St Michael's Church, Brent Knoll (2001) *John G Page*
Brent Knoll Methodist Church, 1837 – 1987, (1987) *Margaret Trapp*
St Mary's Church, East Brent, A Short History (2007) *Penelope Harris*
St Michael's Church, Brent Knoll (2007) *leaflet published by the Parochial Church Council*
Bench Ends, St Michael's Church (2007) *leaflet published by the Parochial Church Council*

An Account of the Easter Rising of 1645 in South Brent during the Civil War (2000) *booklet relating to the John Somerset Memorial in St Michael's Church, Peter M Synge*
Fifty Years at East Brent, The Letters of George Anthony Denison, 1845 – 1896 (1902) *Edited Louisa Evelyn Denison*
Notes of My Life, 1805 – 1878 (1878) *George Anthony Denison*
George Anthony Denison, The Firebrand, 1805 – 1896 (1984) *Joyce Coombs*
Journal of a Somerset Rector, 1803 – 1834, John Skinner (1971) *Edited Howard and Peter Coombs*
The Archaeology of Somerset (2007) *Edited Chris Webster and Tom Mayberry*
Prehistory of the Somerset Levels (1982) *J M Coles and B J Orme*
Worlebury, The story of the Iron Age hill-fort at Weston-super-Mare (1980) *Jane Evans*
Worlebury Hillfort, Weston-super-Mare (1987) *Woodspring Museum Resource Pack*
Aspects of hillfort and hill-top settlement in Somerset in the first to eighth centuries AD (1979) *PhD thesis, Ian Burrow*
Roman Somerset (2001) *Peter Leach*
The Roman Baths and Museum *Official guidebook to Roman Baths at Bath*
Somerset in Domesday (1986) *Robert Dunning*
The Draining of the Somerset Levels (1970) *Michael Williams*
The Severn Estuary, Landscape Evolution and Wetland Reclamation (1997) *Stephen Rippon*
The Early History of Glastonbury, An Edition, Translation and Study of William of Malmesbury's *De Antiquitate Glastonie Ecclesie* (1981) *John Scott*
Arthur: The King in the West (1990) *R W Dunning*
The Composite Manor of Brent, a study of a Large Wetland-Edge Estate up to 1350 (1997) *PhD thesis, J D Harrison*
Aspects of Agrarian Society in Brent Marsh, Somerset, 1500 – 1700 (1981) *PhD thesis, Patricia E C Croot*
The Wealth and Estates of Glastonbury Abbey at the Dissolution in 1539 (2003) *Peter Clery*
The Preparations in Somerset against the Spanish Armada, 1558 – 1588 (1888) *Emanuel Green*
Certificate of Musters in the County of Somerset, AD 1569 (1904) *Emanuel Green, Somerset Record Society Vol XX*
A true report of certain wonderful overflowings of waters in Somerset, Norfolk and other parts of England, AD 1607 (1884) *Edited Ernest E Baker*
Somerset Enclosure Acts and Awards (1948) *W E Tate*
Victorian Somerset, Farming (1979) *Ann Heeley and Martyn Brown*
Kelly's Post Office Directory of Somersetshire, 1861 *Kelly and Co*
The history and antiquities of the County of Somerset (1791) *John Collinson*
A History of Somerset (1983) *Robert Dunning*

Aspects of Somerset History (1973) *T J Hunt and R R Sellman*
"…Bogs and Inundations…" *Iain Miles*
Somerset Brick and Tile Manufacturers, A Brief History and Gazetteer (2000) *Brian J Murless*
Weston-super-Mare, A History and Guide (1988) *Philip Beisly*
Weston-super-Mare in watercolours, an alternative guide (2001) *Rosie and Howard Smith*
A Somerset Childhood (1989) *Phyllis Wyatt*
Somerset Legends (1973) *Berta Lawrence*

General

The Geology of Britain, an Introduction (2009) *Peter Toghill*
Book of the British Countryside (1973) *Published by the AA*
Field Guide to the Butterflies and Other Insects of Britain (2002) *Reader's Digest*
The Wild Flowers of Britain and Northern Europe (1978) *R Fitter, A Fitter, M Blamey*
The Oxford Companion to Family and Local History (2008) *Edited David Hey*
The Oxford Illustrated History of Britain (1985) *Edited Kenneth O Morgan*
A Little History of the English Country Church (2007) *Roy Strong*
English Parish Churches (1993) *Graham Hutton, Olive Cook*
The Journal of the Rev John Wesley A. M. in Four Volumes, Vol III (1827) *Published and Sold by J. Kershaw*
Britain BC (2004) *Francis Pryor*
Britain AD (2005) *Francis Pryor*
Iron Age Britain (2004) *Barry Cunliffe*
Danebury: Anatomy of an Iron Age hillfort (1986) *Barry Cunliffe*
Danebury: The Story of an Iron Age Hill Fort *Barry Cunliffe*
A History of Roman Britain (2001) *Peter Salway*
Roman Britain (2006) *Guy de la Bédoyère*
Alfred the Great, Asser's Life of King Alfred and other contemporary sources (2004) *Simon Keynes and Michael Lapidge*
The Anglo-Saxon Chronicles (2000) *Translated and edited Michael Swanton*
Domesday: The inquest and the book (2000) *David Roffe*
Domesday Book and the Local Historian *Philip Morgan*
Life in a Medieval Village (1991) *Frances and Joseph Gies*
Everyday Life in Medieval England (1994) *Christopher Dyer*
Standards of Living in the later Middle Ages (1998) *Christopher Dyer*
Feudal Britain (1967) *G W S Barrow*
England under the Tudors *G R Elton*
Fire over England, The Armada Beacons *Frank Kitchen*

Websites

A large number of websites have been useful from which I have selected the following few:

Brent Knoll village: *http://www.brentknollvillage.info*
East Brent village: *http://www.rooksbridge.org.uk/east_brent_parish.htm*
Burnham-on-Sea: *http://www.burnham-on-sea.com*
Bridgwater: *http://www.bridgwatertown.com*
Brean Down: *http://www.burnham-on-sea.com/breandown.shtml*
Somerset Historic Environment Record: *http://webapp1.somerset.gov.uk/her/text.asp*
Somerset Heritage Centre (formerly Somerset Record Office): *http://www1.somerset.gov.uk/archives*
National Archives: *http://www.nationalarchives.gov.uk*
Domesday Book: *http://www.domesdaybook.co.uk*
Medieval farming year in the village of Witheridge: *http://www.witheridge-historical-archive.com/medieval-year.htm*
Medieval village of Yalding and medieval history generally: *http://www.spartacus.schoolnet.co.uk/Yalding.htm*
Luttrell Psalter: *http://www.bl.uk/collections/treasures/luttrell/luttrell_broadband.htm*
Great Flood of 1607: *http://website.lineone.net/~mike.kohnstamm/flood*
Slit trenches and defence of Britain: *http://ads.ahds.ac.uk/catalogue/specColl/dob*